The Literature of Cinema

ADVISORY EDITOR: **MARTIN S. DWORKIN**
INSTITUTE OF PHILOSOPHY AND POLITICS OF EDUCATION
TEACHER'S COLLEGE, COLUMBIA UNIVERSITY

THE LITERATURE OF CINEMA presents
a comprehensive selection from the multitude
of writings about cinema, rediscovering materials on its origins, history, theoretical prin-
ciples and techniques, aesthetics, economics,
and effects on societies and individuals. Included are works of inherent, lasting merit
and others of primarily historical significance.
These provide essential resources for serious
study and critical enjoyment of the "magic
shadows" that became one of the decisive cul-
tural forces of modern times.

The Content
of Motion Pictures

Edgar Dale

ARNO PRESS & THE NEW YORK TIMES

New York • 1970

Reprint Edition 1970 by Arno Press Inc.
Library of Congress Catalog Card Number: 77-124026
ISBN 0-405-01644-1
ISBN for complete set: 0-405-01600-X
Manufactured in the United States of America

THE CONTENT OF MOTION PICTURES

MOTION PICTURES AND YOUTH

THE PAYNE FUND STUDIES

W. W. CHARTERS, CHAIRMAN

MOTION PICTURES AND YOUTH: A SUMMARY, by W. W. Charters, Director, Bureau of Educational Research, Ohio State University.

Combined with

GETTING IDEAS FROM THE MOVIES, by P. W. Holaday, Indianapolis Public Schools, and George D. Stoddard, Director, Iowa Child Welfare Research Station.

MOTION PICTURES AND THE SOCIAL ATTITUDES OF CHILDREN, by Ruth C. Peterson and L. L. Thurstone, Department of Psychology, University of Chicago.

Combined with

THE SOCIAL CONDUCT AND ATTITUDES OF MOVIE FANS, by Frank K. Shuttleworth and Mark A. May, Institute of Human Relations, Yale University.

THE EMOTIONAL RESPONSES OF CHILDREN TO THE MOTION PICTURE SITUATION, by W. S. Dysinger and Christian A. Ruckmick, Department of Psychology, State University of Iowa.

Combined with

MOTION PICTURES AND STANDARDS OF MORALITY, by Charles C. Peters, Professor of Education, Pennsylvania State College.

CHILDREN'S SLEEP, by Samuel Renshaw, Vernon L. Miller, and Dorothy Marquis, Department of Psychology, Ohio State University.

MOVIES AND CONDUCT, by Herbert Blumer, Department of Sociology, University of Chicago.

THE CONTENT OF MOTION PICTURES, by Edgar Dale, Research Associate, Bureau of Educational Research, Ohio State University.

Combined with

CHILDREN'S ATTENDANCE AT MOTION PICTURES, by Edgar Dale.

MOVIES, DELINQUENCY, AND CRIME, by Herbert Blumer and Philip M. Hauser, Department of Sociology, University of Chicago.

BOYS, MOVIES, AND CITY STREETS, by Paul G. Cressey and Frederick M. Thrasher, New York University.

HOW TO APPRECIATE MOTION PICTURES, by Edgar Dale, Research Associate, Bureau of Educational Research, Ohio State University.

THE CONTENT OF
MOTION PICTURES

BY

EDGAR DALE

RESEARCH ASSOCIATE, BUREAU OF EDUCATIONAL RESEARCH
OHIO STATE UNIVERSITY

NEW YORK
THE MACMILLAN COMPANY
1935

THIS SERIES OF TWELVE STUDIES OF THE
INFLUENCE OF MOTION PICTURES UPON
CHILDREN AND YOUTH HAS BEEN MADE BY
THE COMMITTEE ON EDUCATIONAL RE-
SEARCH OF THE PAYNE FUND AT THE RE-
QUEST OF THE NATIONAL COMMITTEE FOR
THE STUDY OF SOCIAL VALUES IN MOTION
PICTURES, NOW THE MOTION PICTURE RE-
SEARCH COUNCIL, 366 MADISON AVENUE,
NEW YORK CITY. THE STUDIES WERE DE-
SIGNED TO SECURE AUTHORITATIVE AND
IMPERSONAL DATA WHICH WOULD MAKE
POSSIBLE A MORE COMPLETE EVALUATION
OF MOTION PICTURES AND THEIR SOCIAL
POTENTIALITIES

CHAIRMAN'S PREFACE

MOTION PICTURES are not understood by the present generation of adults. They are new; they make an enormous appeal to children; and they present ideas and situations which parents may not like. Consequently when parents think of the welfare of their children who are exposed to these compelling situations, they wonder about the effect of the pictures upon the ideals and behavior of the children. Do the pictures really influence children in any direction? Are their conduct, ideals, and attitudes affected by the movies? Are the scenes which are objectionable to adults understood by children, or at least by very young children? Do children eventually become sophisticated and grow superior to pictures? Are the emotions of children harmfully excited? In short, just what effect do motion pictures have upon children of different ages?

Each individual has his answer to these questions. He knows of this or that incident in his own experience, and upon these he bases his conclusions. Consequently opinions differ widely. No one in this country up to the present t.me has known in any general and impersonal manner just what effect motion pictures have upon children. Meanwhile children clamor to attend the movies as often as they are allowed to go. Moving pictures make a profound appeal to children of all ages. In such a situation it is obvious that a comprehensive study of the influence of motion pictures upon children and youth is appropr.ate.

To measure these influences the investigators who co-operated to make this series of studies analyzed the problem to discover the most significant questions involved. They set up individual studies to ascertain the answer to the questions and to provide a composite answer to the central question of the nature and extent of these influences. In using this technique the answers must inevitably be sketches without all the details filled in; but when the details are added the picture will not be changed in any essential manner. Parents, educators, and physicians will have little difficulty in fitting concrete details of their own into the outlines which these studies supply.

Specifically, the studies were designed to form a series to answer the following questions: What sorts of scenes do the children of America see when they attend the theaters? How do the mores depicted in these scenes compare with those of the community? How often do children attend? How much of what they see do they remember? What effect does what they witness have upon their ideals and attitudes? Upon their sleep and health? Upon their emotions? Do motion pictures directly or indirectly affect the conduct of children? Are they related to delinquency and crime, and, finally, how can we teach children to discriminate between movies that are artistically and morally good and bad?

The history of the investigations is brief. In 1928 William H. Short, Executive Director of the Motion Picture Research Council, invited a group of university psychologists, sociologists, and educators to meet with the members of the Council to confer about the possibility of discovering just what effect motion pictures have upon children, a subject, as has been indicated, upon which many conflicting opinions and few substantial facts were in existence. The university men proposed a program of study. When Mr. Short appealed to The Payne Fund for a grant to support such an investigation, he found the foundation receptive because of its well-known interest in motion pictures as one of the major influences in the lives of modern youth. When the appropriation had been made the investigators organized themselves into a Committee on Educational Research of The Payne Fund with the following membership: L. L. Thurstone, Frank N. Freeman, R. E. Park, Herbert Blumer, Philip M. Hauser of the University of Chicago; George D. Stoddard, Christian A. Ruckmick, P. W. Holaday, and Wendell Dysinger of the University of Iowa; Mark A. May and Frank K. Shuttleworth of Yale University; Frederick M. Thrasher and Paul G. Cressey of New York University; Charles C. Peters of Pennsylvania State College; Ben D. Wood of Columbia University; and Samuel Renshaw, Edgar Dale, and W. W. Charters of Ohio State University. The investigations have extended through four years, 1929–1932 inclusive.

The committee's work is an illustration of an interesting technique for studying any social problem. The distinctive characteristic of this technique is to analyze a complex social problem into a series of subordinate problems, to select competent investigators to work upon each of the subordinate projects and to integrate the findings of all the investigators as a solution of the initial problem. Such a program yields a skeleton framework, which, while some-what lacking in detail, is substantially correct if the contributing investigations have been validly conducted. To provide this framework or outline is the task of research. To fill in the detail and to provide the interpretations are the natural and easy tasks of those who use the data.

W. W. C.

Ohio State University
June, 1933

AUTHOR'S PREFACE

THIS study, one of the series in the research studies carried out under the auspices of The Payne Fund, aims to discover the content of motion pic ures. The major handicap under which such a study labors is the difficulty of viewing motion pictures after the first few months of their release. A second handicap was the fact that while the content of a motion picture can be described in verbal terms, nevertheless content is a function of the individual who views that particular picture. Fortunately, individuals are conditioned in such a way that in many cases they will react with a high degree of similarity to the same stimulus. Our whole system of language is of course built upon such a premise. Therefore, in spite of the fact of the great necessity for highly detailed studies concerning the nature of content for children and youth of different ages and experiential levels, it is possible for experienced investigators to note verbally the content of motion pictures, and for their results to have a high degree of value. These findings, therefore, are presented not as a complete and final statement of *the* content of motion pictures, but rather as important data on critical questions which parents are asking about the content of motion pictures.

It is the writer's belief that increasingly fine techniques for the study of the content of motion pictures should be developed, and a continuous research program carried out in this field. The motion picture is such a potent factor in the formation of the American public mind that an understanding of the nature of motion picture content is continuously necessary in order to set up adequate forms of social control.

I wish here to acknowledge my indebtedness to the trustees of The Payne Fund for financial support of this undertaking, and to Dr. W. W. Charters for constant assistance in developing the research techniques. The late Mr. W. H. Short, of the Motion Picture Research Council, made many valuable recommendations in the securing of source materials.

Gratitude is here expressed to the major motion picture producing companies which furnished scripts and also newsreel synopses for use in evaluating the content of motion pictures.

For permission to quote from their publications, I also wish to express my appreciation to the authors and publishers mentioned in the following pages.

The study of the themes of 1,500 motion pictures would have been impossible without the generous aid of Mr. P. S. Harrison, 1440 Broadway, New York City, who went to a great deal of trouble to make available his office files of *Harrison's Reports* for the years studied.

I am especially indebted to Miss Hazel Gibbony, of the Bureau of Educational Research, Ohio State University, who for the past four years has been continuously engaged in securing and working on these data.

The techniques for evaluation of themes of 1,500 motion pictures were formulated by Dr. Louis E. Raths, then research assistant at the Bureau of Educational Research. The classification was carried out by Mr. Walter A. Howe. Miss Vivian Weedon, research assistant in the Bureau of Educational Research, Ohio State University, has aided in the preparation of the report, especially in connection with the statistical work.

E. D.

Ohio State University
January, 1935

TABLE OF CONTENTS

LIST OF TABLES

CONTENT OF MOTION PICTURES

CHAPTER I

THE NATURE OF THE STUDY

In 1902 T. L. Talley opened in Los Angeles the first amusement house devoted exclusively to motion pictures.[1] In 1929 it was estimated that there were 77,000,000 weekly attendances at the movies, contributed by about 50,000,-000 people. We have learned in the companion volumes of this series that the information, emotions, attitudes, conduct, and sleep of children and youth are affected by their attendance at motion pictures. We have further learned that the nature of these effects depends upon two factors: (1) the content of the motion pictures viewed, and (2) the way in which these persons reacted to this content.

If children and adults are being affected by what is shown on the screen, it is important that an analysis of motion-picture content be made to show the nature of the stimuli that are producing these changes. Opinions concerning motion-picture content—and there have been literally thousands—range from the bitterest denunciations of the movie fare to the most laudatory commendations. What are the facts?

The purpose of this study, then, is twofold. First, an attempt has been made to devise a method for analyzing the content of motion pictures; and second, the method has

[1] Lewis, Howard T., *The Motion Picture Industry*, New York: D. Van Nostrand Company, 1933, p. 2.

1

been used to discover the content of three different groups of motion pictures.

Analyses of three different intensities were made. The most extensive analysis was that of the major film offerings for the years 1920, 1925, and 1930.[2] Five hundred films from each of these years, virtually the entire product of feature films from the leading producers, were analyzed and classified as to their major theme. This gave us the broad outline of the motion-picture bill of fare. Short written accounts of the stories of these motion pictures were used for this analysis.

This analysis of major themes, which is described in more detail in Chapter II, is valid for presenting the leading ideas with which motion pictures are concerned. It is not valid, however, for answering many of the critical questions which persons are asking concerning the content of motion pictures. In order to obtain a more detailed analysis we viewed 115 motion pictures at the theater. The steps followed in this analysis were these:

1. A canvass was first made of the safeguards which are necessary to ensure fidelity of report when observers are used. Whipple's suggestions for such safeguards[3] were carefully heeded. He states that "If the expectant attention is properly directed, however, the efficiency of observation is very greatly increased."[4] This precaution was observed in this fashion: First of all, the observers familiarized themselves with the story before they went to the theater. The motion-picture reviews in the daily papers usually gave such an account. Reading the story before reviewing the picture gave the investigators a frame of reference, a schema-

[2] In the years 1925 and 1930 it was necessary to fill out the 500 pictures by including some from adjoining years.
[3] Whipple, Guy Montrose, "The Obtaining of Information: Psychology of Observation and Report," *Psychological Bulletin*, XV, 7 (July 1918), pp. 217–248.
[4] *Ibid.*, p. 228.

tized outline which made it possible for them to grasp easily what occurred on the screen. Second, each observer carried a schedule of points on which to secure information. This schedule included the critical areas in which we desired information, and had been worked out in coöperation with the observers. Further, three observers were used on 75 of the 115 films reviewed by this schedule.

The schedule was developed in this fashion:

All available literature dealing with favorable and unfavorable criticisms of theatrical motion pictures was read with a view to determining the positive and negative values which have been stated for such motion pictures. An analysis schedule was developed, based on a classification of these possible values and detriments. The major headings in the final form of this schedule sheet are as follows:

Social Values in Motion Pictures

I. Nature of American Life and Characters
II. Nature of Foreign Life and Characters
III. Motivation of Characters
IV. Emotional Appeals to Audience and Methods of Making Them—The "Kick" of the Movies
V. Crime, Delinquency, and Violence
VI. Relations of Sexes
VII. Military Situations
VIII. Depiction of Underprivileged Peoples
IX. Deportment, Language, Manner and Tone of Voice, Type of Dialogue and Song

Each of these categories was further subdivided. The subdivisions used for Category No. I follow:

I. Nature of American Life and Characters
   A. Home
   B. Education
   C. Religion
   D. Economics

E. Agriculture
F. Industry and commerce
G. Civic life
H. Recreation
I. Social conventions
J. Clothing conventions
K. Narcotics and stimulants
L. Law enforcement
M. American men
N. American women
O. American youth
P. American children

Each of these subcategories was further divided by a series of points; *e.g.:*

F. Industry and Commerce

Pay special attention to the following points:
1. The nature of the portrayal of industrial and commercial activity.
2. Goals of characters engaged in industrial activity.
3. Methods of distribution of goods.
4. Nature of portrayal of owners and workers.
5. Nature of the management of industry.

The reviewer was expected to write on the analysis sheet descriptive details of scenes in the picture which dealt with these points.

2. Accuracy of report was further ensured by following a second warning of Whipple's, *i.e.:* "Whenever any interval of time elapses between the actual carrying out of observation and the recording of it by word or gesture or pen, the accuracy and completeness of the record tends to be reduced by errors of memory." [5]   Each observer recorded at the theater the pertinent material which he was seeing on the

⁵ *Ibid.,* p. 233.

screen. He occupied a seat near a light and it was possible in this way to make satisfactory notes. These notes were written up either that day or the next. Even with these precautions, minor errors were discovered. This situation was met, in part, by observing a third canon set up by Whipple: "When a number of persons report upon the same matter, those details upon which agreement appears may in general be considered as correct." [6]

An analysis of this type makes possible the answering of many important questions concerning motion-picture content. Its deficiency lies in the fact that it does not make available the total context in which each of the situations occurred. We felt, further, that we needed a number of accounts which would present almost completely the entire range of content of a motion picture in the context of the narrative itself. To that end, we secured from the producers dialogue scripts and used them in our analysis of 40 motion pictures. The script contains all the dialogue and enough of the settings and action to give each bit of dialogue its proper chronological order. The observers for these 40 motion pictures were all trained stenographers and the schedules were used as before. What the observers now did was to:

1. Familiarize themselves with the dialogue script before attending the motion picture.

2. Attend the film and take stenographic notes of all materials not included in the dialogue script. This consisted of detailed descriptions of settings, clothing worn, gestures, intonations and facial expressions of characters, approximate age, economic levels, and so on.

3. Immediately write up the picture in the form of a running narrative based upon a combination of the dialogue script and stenographic notes, every change of scene being

6 *Ibid.*, p. 238.

carefully indicated. These reviews averaged approximately forty double-spaced typewritten pages each.

Of the 40 pictures thus reviewed, 27 were viewed by two or more trained observers, the remaining 13 being viewed by one trained observer who had been the research assistant throughout the entire experiment.

The final results of the investigation as far as methodology is concerned are: (1) a reliable technique for the classification of motion pictures according to major theme, (2) a schedule sheet by means of which critical information about motion pictures can be secured by trained observers, and (3) a technique for highly detailed film analysis.

To summarize, then, the technique for evaluation of motion pictures according to major theme was applied to 500 feature pictures in each of the years 1920, 1925, and 1930. The schedule sheet was applied to 75 motion pictures and their content determined through this method. And finally, a highly detailed narrative account was secured through the application of this schedule sheet to 40 additional motion pictures.

SAMPLING PROBLEMS

The problem of sampling, in regard to the pictures, offered a difficult task. It is evident that what we were trying to discover was the content of motion pictures which were attended. In other words, pictures like "Little Women" or "She Done Him Wrong," both of which broke box-office records, should probably receive more weight in a sampling than pictures made by the same company which received scant attendance. However, when we attempted to put this criterion into practice, we soon discovered that little authentic information was made available to the public concerning those pictures which were box-office successes, and beyond a dozen or so pictures which each year are patently successful, one had little data on which to base such a sampling. Further, because of the conditions under which this research had to be carried out, by the time the box-office success of such pictures had been established they would have been drawn out of circulation and it would be almost impossible to find theaters showing them.

Our final conclusion as to choice, therefore, was to make a random selection of pictures. In this random selection an attempt was made to choose pictures from among the various major producers at least roughly in proportion to their total product for that year. For example, in 1930 this meant a heavy selection from Paramount and a relatively light selection from United Artists. This method gives us the best assurance that the total motion-picture product is adequately sampled. Table 1 indicates the proportion of pictures of various types in our selection for analysis as compared with the total production of the major producing companies in 1930.

It will be seen that our random selection of 115 motion pictures approximates remarkably well the entire major production for the year 1930. When one compares the percentages of the 40 pictures classified by the various types with the percentages of the 500 pictures released in 1930, he sees that crime is slightly underemphasized, sex slightly overemphasized, mystery and war slightly overemphasized, and children, history, travel, and comedy each has a slightly higher percentage than in the 1930 productions.

What is motion-picture content? As we have defined it, it constitutes a verbal description of what competent observers say has occurred on the motion-picture screen. Such a description only suggests the possible reaction of individuals to such content. What we describe as the same stimulus

TABLE 1

COMPARISON OF THE RESULTS OF THREE SAMPLINGS OF MOTION PICTURES

Number and per cent of pictures of each type as shown by samples of 500, 115, and 40

Type of Picture	500 Pictures Released in 1930 ᵃ		115 Pictures Analyzed ᵇ		40 Pictures Analyzed in Detail	
	Number	Per cent	Number	Per cent	Number	Per cent
Crime.........	137	27.4	27	23.5	9	22.5
Sex..........	75	15.0	18	15.6	8	20.0
Love.........	148	29.6	34	29.6	7	17.5
Mystery......	24	4.8	4	3.5	3	7.5
War..........	19	3.8	4	3.5	3	7.5
Children......	1	.2	1	.9	1	2.5
History.......	7	1.4	1	.9	1	2.5
Travel........	9	1.8	2	1.7	1	2.5
Comedy......	80	16.0	24	20.9	7	17.5
Social propaganda......	0	0.0	0	0.0	0	0.0
Total........	500	100	115	100	40	100

ᵃ Fifty-two of the 115 pictures analyzed are included in this sample. These 500 pictures represent the total 1930 production.
ᵇ This sample includes the 40 pictures analyzed in detail.

will have varying effects on observers, as has been pointed out by other investigators in these Payne Fund researches. The reader is therefore warned that this study does not deal with the effects of motion pictures on children and youth, except by inference. A study of content deals only with possible effects. These data, then, must be interpreted in the light of other investigations dealing with the actual reactions of children and youth to varying motion-picture content.

The attempt to analyze the content of motion pictures is approached with temerity. For one to attempt to discover just what is contained within the covers of 500 books written in 1920, 1925, and 1930 would certainly provide an extremely difficult problem of analysis. To analyze the content of motion pictures does not seem so difficult, yet it is a stupendous task. Compromises were necessary, of course. To have pulled out all the content of these pictures would have required a lifetime. The aim has been rather to develop a technique, to discover the major themes treated, and then to analyze critically a small sample of pictures in an attempt to note the behavior therein portrayed.

But an analysis of the content of motion pictures does not relieve the writer of the responsibility of giving his judgment about the facts discovered. He has therefore attempted to do this at various points throughout the study. When such judgments have been offered, however, the writer has very pointedly indicated that they represent inferences from the facts stated. Naturally, we may expect that some people will draw different inferences from the same set of facts, because no two people ever interpret the same evidence wholly alike. However, it is the writer's belief that the inferences which he draws from the data are the ones best justified by the facts presented.

SUMMARY

The purpose of this study was twofold: first, to devise a technique for analyzing the content of motion pictures, and second, to discover by this technique what the content of motion pictures has been.

Analyses of three different intensities were made.

The first consisted of virtually the entire product of feature films from the major producers for the years 1920, 1925, and 1930. Five hundred films for each year, making a total of 1,500 films for the three years, were analyzed to discover major themes.

The second consisted of 115 films released as follows: 45 during the year 1929, 46 during the year 1930, and 24 during the year 1931. These films were viewed at the theater by observers and reported by means of a schedule especially prepared for this purpose. The technique of observation was based upon Whipple's studies. Each observer read a review before attending the theater. He recorded pertinent comments at the theater and wrote the complete report immediately after viewing the film. This level of analysis is referred to in tables as "the 115 pictures."

The third level consisted of 40 of the 115 films used for the second-level analysis. This level was the most detailed analysis. A dialogue script of each picture was obtained from the producer. The observers familiarized themselves with this script before attending the picture, took stenographic notes on points not covered by the script while viewing the film, and wrote up the results in the form of a running narrative. This level of analysis is referred to in the tables as "the 40 pictures."

CHAPTER II
THE GENERAL THEMES OF 1,500 MOTION PICTURES

THE methods used to analyze films for their general themes must depend, of course, upon the type of evidence available regarding such content. It is possible only at great expense to view films even a year old. Therefore, studies of the content of pictures produced in the past must, except under unusual circumstances, be based upon written accounts of such stories—reviews, synopses, and so on.

The investigator discovered that the best source of information concerning pictures produced in the past was *Harrison's Reports*,[1] a reviewing service to exhibitors which reviews all the important feature releases of the independent as well as the major producing companies, furnishing a short account of the story of the film and a statement of its probable box-office value. The accuracy of these stories was validated by comparing them with other written accounts and with accounts of motion pictures which the investigators had viewed. We decided to make our study one of the general content of 500 feature pictures released in each of the years 1920, 1925, and 1930.[2] This represents the total output of feature pictures released in these years by the major producing organizations, as well as the important feature releases of the independent producers.

The basis assumed for the classification of picture types was the major theme of the picture. As applied to motion

[1] *Harrison's Reports*, 1440 Broadway, New York City.
[2] In the years 1925 and 1930 it was necessary to fill out the 500 pictures by including some from adjoining years.

11

pictures, the term "major theme" was interpreted to mean the subject matter of the play, the nature of the activity around which the play revolves, that which is given the greatest prominence, the central tendency of the movie, or the general impression of the motion picture upon the observer. In other words, the classification sought was one which would answer the question, "What kind of movie was it?"

Objection may be taken to the hypothesis that motion pictures do have definite themes. It is true that in some cases the theme is difficult to classify. Our experience has shown, however, that the majority of pictures do have a discernible theme and that, with the proper outline to follow, different observers will classify the picture similarly. With regard to a certain portion of the movies, however, there seems to be no central stem, no general idea, no vehicle to which the situations and incidents in the play are attached. In these pictures there is often little continuity between successive episodes and, as has been stated, there is no organic unity of the whole picture; no single type of activity seems outstanding. The pictures are compounded of many types of activity—criminal, sexual, comic, romantic, and otherwise. These pictures which do not have a definite theme represent but a very small portion of all movies released.

The first problem in classifying pictures is one of definition. One must define what is meant by a crime picture, a sex picture, a war picture, and so on. When there is agreement upon definitions it is reasonable to suppose that different observers will be highly consistent among themselves in the results of their separate classifications.

Definition and classification of pictures will depend upon the use which is to be made of the data. Terms must be so defined as to be usable by those people who will have need of them. Individuals who ultimately will make use of these definitions and the scheme for classifying must understand the present use of them. We may expect, then, that they will arrive at conclusions which are highly similar; that is, if a number of people follow identical methods and use identical data, their classifications and enumerations should be highly consistent. Critics who accept these definitions will accept the findings; critics who reject the definitions will refuse to accept the findings.

The data on themes were secured by reading each of the 1,500 reviews listed by Harrison and indicating the general reaction of the reader to the story accounts. If, upon completing the review, the reader's general impression of the movie was, "It is a crime picture," he classified it under the major theme labeled *crime*. One further step was then taken: the reader was asked to indicate the type of crime picture which it exemplified. All pictures thus received a double classification: First, each picture was classified as to a major theme; then, after having been so classified, it was further defined as a particular type of movie under its appropriate theme.

The classification outline was not prepared in advance of the reading of *Harrison's Reports*. Two hundred reviews were first read and an experimental, tentative outline was prepared. At first the classification expanded rapidly. After these 200 films had been classified and the main outline of the classification had been formed, the growth was slow. If and when a distinctly new type was encountered, the classification was enlarged to care for it. There were many changes made in this preliminary draft, wholly in the light of the use to which the data were subsequently to be put, and in the hope of developing an outline which when used by many readers would yield high similarity in results.

The next question to be raised deals with the value of the results. Any person or group of persons may devise a scheme of classification of motion pictures, but if their conclusions vary greatly among other intelligent persons or groups the value of the results is diminished considerably and they are unacceptable to interested individuals. On the other hand, if the scheme of classification is such as to yield uniform results when it is employed by intelligent individuals, then the conclusions have value, particularly if those conclusions focus upon the important questions which are raised in that field.

One person was selected to read 500 motion pictures released in 1920. With the aid of the outline he classified each of the 500 pictures, both as to type and as to a particular kind under the appropriate type. When he had completed his work, 100 titles were selected at random from the 500, and two other readers were asked to classify this number, with the same outline as a guide.

There was perfect agreement among the three readers in 87 out of the 100 pictures as to the type of movie—crime, sex, and so on. The same procedure was followed with respect to 100 movies issued in 1925. For that year there was perfect agreement among the three readers in 86 out of 100 cases. Employing the same technique for 100 pictures released in 1930, there was perfect agreement among the three readers in 88 out of 100 pictures.

This is a perfect agreement in approximately nine cases in every ten. The technique was considered a very satisfactory one for our purpose, which was to classify motion pictures according to main types.

The outline, when completed, contained pictures centering around ten major themes. Altogether, 1,500 reviews were read and all of them were classified among these ten headings. The complete outline, including the types to be found under each major theme, is included here. It should be pointed out that this classification and outline was developed for the purpose of classifying the general themes of motion pictures when they are presented in a short review of the picture. It will need modification when used with other types of data. The subclassifications are not assumed to be either complete or mutually exclusive.

Classification of Motion Pictures

I. Crime
   1. Blackmailing; extortion.
   2. Injury, hate, and revenge—idea of vengeance—feuds.
   3. Corruption in politics or business; bribery; swindling. Abuse of constituted authority, misuse of office.
   4. Underworld melodrama; crook plays; criminal activity predominant. Racketeers, bootleggers, gamblers, gangsters, smugglers, thieves.
   5. Outlaws, bandits, rustlers—"Western" type—holdups, gun fighting, etc., main interest.
   6. About criminal types and activities—prison stories.

II. Sex
   1. Emphasis upon living together without marriage.
   2. Loose living, impropriety known or implied; plot revolving around seduction, adultery, kept women; illegitimate children the central characters.
   3. No sexual impropriety but sex is the theme; sex situations, "woman for sale" stuff.
   4. Bedroom farce; incidents are farcical but it is a play on fringes of sexual impropriety.

III. Love
   1. Love against a background of thrills, suspense, melodrama.
   2. Courtship, love, flirtations, marital difficulties.
   3. Historical romance.
   4. Operetta type, colorful scenes, songs.
   5. Character portrayal—love interest present but not dominant.[3]

---

[3] In the case of two or three pictures this classification under *love* was unsatisfactory. No new category was developed because of the scarcity of this type of film.

IV. Mystery
    1. Murder mystery type—thrills, horrors, detective stories.
    2. Vampires. Ghosts.
    3. Life after death, reincarnation, emphasis on weirdness.

V. War
    1. Spying, secret service in war, suspense, thrills.
    2. Characters are soldiers; life as soldiers, actual scenes of warfare minimized.
    3. Characters are soldiers; actual scenes of destructive warfare, bombing, killing, and fighting predominate.

VI. Children
    1. Plays designed primarily for children, or plays in which children are the central characters.

VII. History
    1. The westward movement.
    2. Reconstruction and expansion after the Civil War.
    3. Historical in setting and characters.

VIII. Exploration—Travel—Animal
    1. Pictures of the type involving polar and other explorations, travels, and ones in which animals are central characters.

IX. Comedy
    1. High comedy, light comedy-drama, humorous side predominant.
    2. Farce, incidents presented in a farcical way.
    3. Low comedy, slapstick, vulgarity, "pie-throwing" type.
    4. Musical comedy type. Plot secondary to music.

X. Social Propaganda
    1. Labor troubles, race suicide, socialism, Bolshevism, Americanization, radicalism, patriotism, etc.

The data sheet which was used for this study is reproduced in Appendix I.

In making the classification and the distribution, the judgment of the reviewer for *Harrison's Reports* was usually accepted if the facts concerning the picture did not conflict with the classification. In most cases, however, *Harrison's Reports* did not classify the picture, and the classifier had to decide on the theme by reading the review. Occasionally a clue as to the major theme of the picture is given,

TABLE 2

COMPARISON OF THE TYPES OF MOTION PICTURES PRODUCED IN 1920, 1925, AND 1930

Number and per cent of pictures of each type as shown by a 500 sample each year

Type of Picture	Release Date					
	1920		1925		1930	
	Number	Per cent	Number	Per cent	Number	Per cent
Crime.......	120	24.0	148	29.6	137	27.4
Sex..........	65	13.0	84	16.8	75	15.0
Love.........	223	44.6	164	32.8	148	29.6
Mystery......	16	3.2	11	2.2	24	4.8
War..........	10	2.0	11	2.2	19	3.8
Children......	2	.4	4	.8	1	.2
History.......	0	0.0	6	1.2	7	1.4
Travel........	1	.2	7	1.4	9	1.8
Comedy......	59	11.8	63	12.6	80	16.0
Social propaganda......	4	.8	2	.4	0	0.0
Total........	500	100	500	100	500	100

as when a picture is described as a "Crook Play," an "Underworld Melodrama," a "Mystery Play," a "Musical Comedy," or some other characteristic not unlike these. In such cases the hint was helpful, but the classifier had to make the final decision according to the written review in all its aspects.

With methods which yield results of a highly uniform nature, what proportion of all movies does each of the types represent? The total number of each type for each of the three periods and the percentage of all pictures released which each type represents are summarized and presented in Table 2.

A word of caution must be inserted here with respect to the interpretation of these data. The reader is urged to keep in mind the definition of each of the major themes, and to remember that a picture that has *love* for its major theme may contain scenes of criminality. Crime, and sometimes much crime, occurs in mystery pictures, war pictures, pictures dealing with sex, and even in comedies. Therefore, when it is said that 24 per cent of the motion pictures released in 1920 represent *crime* pictures, it means that 24 per cent of the pictures had a major theme of crime. In other words, the enumeration really underestimates the amount of criminality shown on the screen. In the same manner the percentage of sex in motion pictures is underestimated since incidents dealing with sex—and sometimes these include sexual impropriety—are found in the pictures classified under categories other than sex. They are placed in the category bearing this title only when the major theme of the picture was sexual in nature. In other words, the data submitted in the present report are very conservative in nature.

NATURE OF THE EVIDENCE CONCERNING CONTENT

The following facts can be gleaned from Table 2. We note, first of all, that there was an increase in the number of crime pictures produced in 1925. The number decreases in 1930, although the number of crime pictures produced in 1930 is still greater than that produced in 1920. When we consider the disagreement of 13 per cent [4] in the judgment of those classifying the films, however, small increases of this size may not be statistically significant. Sex pictures comprised 13 per cent in 1920, 16.8 per cent in 1925, and 15 per cent in 1930.

[4] It will be remembered that there was perfect agreement in 87, 86, and 88 pictures out of 100 respectively for the years 1920, 1925, and 1930. The per cent of disagreement was therefore 13, 14, and 12.

Perhaps the most striking shift in production is the one in pictures classified under *love*. These are stories of romance. We see that 44.6 per cent of the pictures were so classified in 1920, 32.8 in 1925, and only 29.6 in 1930.

Mystery pictures are relatively small in number, and make only slight shifts. We do note, however, the effect of the "horror" cycle in the increase from 11 mystery pictures in 1925 to 24 in 1930.

The paucity of children's pictures is clearly indicated by the fact that 2 such pictures were released in 1920, 4 in 1925, and 1 in 1930. This should not be interpreted, however, as meaning that this represents the total number of pictures fitted for children. A study such as this does not indicate whether a picture in this category or in any of the other categories is desirable or undesirable for children. The classification *children* must be interpreted in terms of the definition set forth on page 16.

The number of pictures that can be classified as *history* is small, as is that of *travel* and *social propaganda*. *Comedy*, however, apparently is on the increase, with a greater number of comedy pictures in 1930 than in 1925 and more in 1925 than in 1920. The increase in comedy pictures may be attributed in part to the introduction of sound motion pictures, making it possible to film musical comedies.

It is evident from these figures that crime, sex, and love pictures constitute the major bulk of the production, being 81.6 per cent in 1920, 79.2 per cent in 1925, and 72 per cent in 1930. The chances, therefore, are three out of four that an individual who selects his movies wholly at random will see a crime, sex, or love picture. When we consider crime and sex together, we get very clear evidence that there has been an increase in the number of pictures which can be classified in this category—37 per cent in 1920, 46.4 per cent in 1925, and 42.4 per cent in 1930.

Other details concerning the content of motion pictures may prove of interest here. It is evident that the love theme dominates and has the largest single percentage of pictures. However, almost as many pictures deal with crime. The percentage of pictures that can be classified as sex pictures represent on the whole about one seventh of the annual production. A child who attends motion pictures indiscriminately will have one opportunity in seven of seeing what we have defined as a sex picture. The chance of seeing a crime picture is about one in four; that of seeing a love picture about one in three. The remaining percentage of pictures is divided among pictures of mystery, war, children, history, travel, comedy, and social propaganda.

SUMMARY

Fifteen hundred motion pictures released during the years 1920, 1925, and 1930 were used for this study of major themes. Their major themes were classified into ten types: *love, crime, comedy, sex, mystery, war, travel, history, children, social propaganda.* Each of these types was carefully defined. The classification was built up during the reading of the reviews.

In order to check the accuracy of the classification, 100 pictures selected at random from each of the three groups of 500 pictures released in the years 1920, 1925, and 1930 were classified by three persons. The average per cent of agreement was 87.

Acquaintanceship with the type definition is essential to an understanding of the conclusions. In 1930 the largest proportion of pictures fell in the *love* classification, though *crime* ran *love* a close second. *Comedy* was third in rank and *sex* fourth. There was a decided break between the per cent of pictures classified as *sex* and the next in rank, *mystery*. The other classifications in rank order were *war*, *travel*, *history*, *children*, and *social propaganda*. No picture released in 1930 was classified under the last in rank, *social propaganda*.

There was an increase in the per cent of 1930 pictures over 1920 pictures in the following categories: *comedy*, *crime*, *sex*, *mystery*, *history*, and *travel*, while there was a decrease in *love*, *children*, and *social propaganda*. The most marked change was in *love*, which fell from 44.6 per cent in 1920 to 29.6 per cent in 1930.

What proportion of the pictures should be devoted to each of these categories? Are there some areas, now being entirely neglected by the motion pictures, which might well be included with these categories? Considering the present allotment of pictures in each category, what attitude should be taken toward the attendance at the movies of children? of adolescents? In the light of the findings of other studies in this series as to the effect of the motion pictures upon sleep and actions, what is the significance of a movie bill of fare which provides in 5 pictures, 2 dealing with *crime* or *sex*, 2 dealing with *comedy or romantic love*, and the remaining 1 with either *mystery*, *war*, *children*, *history*, or *travel?*

To the writer, such a distribution points to the need for careful parental supervision in the selection of motion pictures. Children can undoubtedly spend their time more profitably and enjoyably than in watching pictures dealing with these mature and probably, to them, uninteresting problems.

With adolescents the answer is not so easy. The movies seem a logical place in which the adolescent may become acquainted with some of the problems which he will face as an adult. If these problems are realistically and truthfully presented they may aid in the solution of life problems to come. On the other hand, adolescence is likely to be a time of instability and one in which the individual is unusually susceptible to influence. Those who are interested in guiding the coming generation must pay attention to these influences.

For adults? The answer here depends upon one's conception of the purpose of the movies. The emphasis on *romantic love* and *comedy* points to escape from everyday life as a major function of the movies. Escape is undoubtedly one of the purposes of the movies. Is it sufficiently important to justify the emphasis it is given? Is it socially desirable?

The fact that two fifths of the pictures are concerned with *crime* and *sex* indicate a belief that a purpose of the movies is to deal with life problems and their solution. Certainly these are two problems that are always with us. Are they sufficiently important to warrant the attention they are receiving? Are there not other problems which might well be handled on the screen? Would not the motion-picture medium be a good one in which to present government, commerce, or industry? Are there no social problems other than those of crime and sex which would lend themselves to dramatic treatment?

In addition to the question of the desirable proportion to be included in each category, there is the important question of how the subjects that are considered are treated. The answer to this question will be sought in the following chapters.

CHAPTER III

LOCALES AND SETTINGS OF MOTION PICTURES

THROUGH the locales, and settings of motion pictures it becomes possible to reveal to the viewer a wide range of geographical settings and human habitations. The presentation of a variety of locales and settings can provide individuals an insight into living conditions the world over. By this means such verbal symbols as *the American Rockies, the Alps, African jungles, Arabian deserts, Eskimo huts, straw-thatched African villages, the palaces of the Indian princes,* are given life and vitality. Through diversity and accuracy in settings, individuals can widely expand the range and depth of their experience. Thus they may gain an understanding of the varying conditions under which people live, and develop sympathy for differences which result from such variations.

It is evident, therefore, that the content of a motion picture cannot be studied apart from the settings—the locales—of the picture. Indeed, the background against which the story is projected provides a vital part of the total effect of the play upon the observer. The background gives a mental set by means of which the observer interprets what occurs on the screen. For example, when the early flashes of a motion picture indicate that the scenes are laid in the Sahara, at once we expect to see the action of the play conditioned by the climate, the weather, or the topography of this area. We are mentally prepared to see camels, sandstorms, Arabs,

French Foreign Legions; and the logic of the play is not disturbed by their presence.

The background, then, puts us in a state of expectant attention for certain customary accompaniments of typical settings. A Western locale will lead us to expect the content to deal with outdoor life, cowboys, ranchers, horseback riders. A sophisticated interior will lead us to expect a society drama, with much of the material projected against a background of interiors.

This brief introduction will serve to give point to our study of locales and settings. We have attempted in this study to obtain information concerning a series of problems dealing with the locales and settings in which motion pictures are laid. The answer has been secured through a search directed by the following questions:

1. What is the relative proportion of exterior sets to interior sets? What sets are included under each?
2. How diverse are the backgrounds against which motion-picture stories are projected? Do we see both town and country? Do the sets include foreign countries as well as the United States?
3. How meaningful are the sets used? In other words, if a foreign set is presented does it really give much of the background of the country, or is it highly conventionalized?
4. What is the economic character of the settings? Are they those which suggest wealth, luxury, and splendor, or the reverse?
5. Are the locales and settings diverse not only geographically but also in terms of industrial and commercial activities? Are certain settings portraying specialized groups much more frequently used than others?

LOCALES

Types of Locale

Tables 3 and 4 show the type and frequency of locale used in the 115 motion pictures which were viewed at the theater.

Table 3 shows the type of locale and frequency of occurrence of each type or combination of types. The three major categories are: United States, foreign, and indeterminate. The classifications "United States" and "foreign" are self-explanatory. "Indeterminate" locale includes such categories as aboard a ship at sea, an imaginary kingdom, an imaginary island, and so on. Table 4 gives the most frequent specific locales.

Seventy-three per cent of all the pictures are laid either entirely or partially in the United States. Of these, 54.8 per cent are located entirely in this country, and the remaining

TABLE 3

UNITED STATES AND FOREIGN LOCALES WHICH WERE SHOWN IN THE
115 PICTURES

Number and per cent of pictures in which each type of locale was seen

Locale	Number	Per cent
United States (entirely)	63	54.8
Foreign (entirely)	24	20.9
United States and Foreign	16	13.9
Indeterminate	3	2.6
United States and Indeterminate	3	2.6
Foreign and Indeterminate	4	3.5
United States—Foreign—Indeterminate	2	1.7
Total	115	100

18.2 per cent is distributed as follows: 13.9 in both the United States and some foreign country; 2.6 in the United States and an indeterminate locale; and 1.7 in a locale including the United States, a foreign country, and an indeterminate locale.

Forty per cent of the 115 pictures had a locale either wholly or partly foreign. Pictures with an entirely foreign locale comprised 20.9 per cent, and the remaining 19.1 per cent is made up of the following combinations: United States and foreign, 13.9; foreign and indeterminate locale, 3.5; United States, foreign, and indeterminate, 1.7.

The total percentage of pictures involving indeterminate locales is 10.4. Of this, 2.6 represents pictures with entirely indeterminate locales, and the remaining 7.8 is distributed as follows: United States and indeterminate, 2.6; foreign and indeterminate, 3.5; United States, foreign, and indeterminate, 1.7.

TABLE 4

SPECIFIC LOCALES WHICH WERE SEEN IN 3 OR MORE OF THE 115 PICTURES

Number of pictures in which each locale was shown

Locale United States	Number	Locale Foreign	Number	Locale Indeterminate	Number
New York City...	37	Paris.........	11	Aboard ship at	
Large city.......	13	London........	8	sea..........	14
Western United		Mexico........	5	Imaginary island	3
States........	9	South America .	4		
Indeterminate....	7	English country	4		
California........	5	Russia........	4		
Florida..........	4	England (gen.) .	3		
Texas...........	3	French village..	3		
Small town......	3				

Most Frequent Locales

The five most common United States locales in order of frequency (see Table 4), are New York City, "a large city," Western United States, indeterminate, and California. The six most common foreign locales in order of frequency are Paris, London, Mexico, South America, English country, and Russia. The most common indeterminate locale is aboard a ship at sea.

Table 5 calls attention to the most frequent general locales.

The six following groups account for 73.2 per cent of all general locales: Eastern United States, 22.8 per cent; General

United States, 14.0 per cent; Western United States, 10.9 per cent; France, 10.4 per cent; England, 7.8 per cent; and aboard a ship at sea, 7.3 per cent.

TABLE 5

General Locales Seen Most Frequently in the 115 Pictures

Number and per cent of pictures in which each type of locale was shown and number and per cent of locales of each type

Locale	Locales		Pictures	
	Number	Per cent	Number	Per cent
Eastern United States........	44	22.8	44	38.3
General United States........	27	14.0	27	23.5
Western United States.......	21	10.9	21	18.3
France....................	20	10.4	20	17.4
England..................	15	7.8	15	13.0
Ship at sea................	14	7.3	14	12.2
Total.....................	141	73.2		
Other locales..............	52	26.9		
Grand total...............	193	100		

When these locales are further analyzed in Table 6, a distinctly metropolitan trend is discovered. Thirty-eight per cent of all locales are metropolitan. This urban tendency is even more striking when United States locales are separated from foreign. Data not shown on the table indicate that 52 per cent of all United States locales were metropolitan and were divided among New York City, 35 per cent; an indeterminate large city, 12 per cent; the remaining 5 per cent was made up of 2 locales of San Francisco, and 1 each of Atlantic City, Washington, D. C., Detroit, and New Orleans. The tendency to show metropolitan areas is less noticeable with the foreign locales as only 28 per cent of these were found to be metropolitan. Paris accounted for 16 per cent of these locales; London, for 11 per cent; and Havana, for 1 per cent.

TABLE 6

METROPOLITAN LOCALES IN THE 115 PICTURES

Number and per cent of the locales which were metropolitan

Locale	Number	Per cent
United States:		
New York City	37	19
An indeterminate large city	13	7
Specific large cities [a]	6	3
Foreign:		
Paris	10	5
London	7	3.5
Havana	1	.5
Total	74	38

[a] The cities which make up this group are: San Francisco, 2; Atlantic City, 1; Washington, D. C., 1; New Orleans, 1; Detroit, 1.

What do these data mean? Do they suggest that a motion picture which has a majority of its locales in metropolitan areas is contributing, with other agencies, to the urbanization of our population? The extensive use of the large city as a locale may be deliberate on the part of the producer or it may just have happened. Some persons would maintain that the glamour of the big city brings in the customers in the rural areas. Others would just as stoutly defend the thesis that the rural population is relatively uninterested in the goings-on in the big cities. No evidence on either side of the question appears to be available at the present time. However, while the rural groups are gaining some notion, often incorrect, of urban life, little attention was given in these 115 pictures to rural life, excepting of course certain of the inaccurate but glamorous ideas of ranching life in the West.

Foreign Locales

It will be noted that a significant proportion of the 115 motion pictures have foreign locations. On the face of it, this might appear to demonstrate that through the viewing of motion pictures one gets an adequate insight into the physical settings of foreign lands. On the other hand, it is possible that these foreign settings are very meager as far as their adequacy of portrayal of physical setting is concerned. What are the facts? A statement follows relative to the foreign settings in the 40 motion pictures which we studied in detail. (See Chapter I, pages 5 and 6, for a description of this technique.) The following list shows the foreign country or countries represented in each of the 17 pictures containing foreign locales:

Picture No. 1. England
"   "   2. Hawaii
"   "   3. Russia
"   "   4. England
"   "   5. Cuba, South America
"   "   6. France
"   "   7. Antarctica
"   "   8. Austria, Russia
"   "   9. France
"   "   10. France
"   "   11. Monaco, Indeterminate Foreign
"   "   12. Morocco
"   "   13. Sumatra
"   "   14. Russia
"   "   15. Mexico
"   "   16. Mexico, Monaco, Spain, France, England
"   "   17. England, France

The first part of Picture No. 1 is laid in London, but the audience is given only a glimpse of a few exterior and interior settings which might have been located almost anywhere. The locale of the picture then shifts to an English country estate, and here more typically English scenes and landscape are presented, although only a few of the scenes take place outside the limits of two large estates. We do see, however, a country road and some of the countryside.

Picture No. 2, which has its setting in Hawaii, gives the viewer some very beautiful and representative shots of that part of the world. We are shown the sea and the beach, a glimpse of a large hotel with its surrounding grounds, a country road on the island. The Hawaiian atmosphere is effectively presented.

Picture No. 3 includes quite a bit of the Russian country and atmosphere. We see an isolated German prison camp in a Russian forest, snow-covered, bitter cold. A prisoner escapes and we follow him to a hut in the snowy forest. Later we are shown a small Russian town, with snowy streets, along which sleighs jingle. Church bells are ringing, and we see the picturesquely dressed peasants.

Although most of Picture No. 4 is laid in England, it is the England of King Arthur's time. We see several pictures of the countryside, one scene in a forest, some of the estate about the King's castle, and the castle of Morgan le Fay. One's general impression of England, as gleaned from this picture, however, would be somewhat vague.

Picture No. 5 is laid mostly on the high seas, although it does give a few glimpses of towns at which the ship stops. We see a little of Havana, but nothing extensive except a street or two and the interior of a café. There is, however, a quite adequate presentation of Orambo, a little, hot, dreary town some place on the coast of South America.

Picture No. 6 is laid in France at the time of Napoleon's downfall. We see little of France, however, beyond interiors such as an inn, a prison, a chateau. There is a brief shot of the grounds about the chateau, a road, and a woods where the hero and heroine go horseback riding.

The scenes from Picture No. 7, which is laid in the Antarctic, give an admirable picture of that part of the world. We see not only the conditions under which the men live, but also the hazards that the weather and the terrain present to the explorers in their dash for the South Pole. Great care had evidently been taken in order to make the Antarctic scenes seem realistic. We are shown the snow dugouts, the great mountains of ice which make the approach to the Pole so difficult; and we are made to realize the extreme cold, the icy wind.

Picture No. 8, laid in Austria and Russia, consists almost entirely of interior scenes, and those not particularly representative ones, with the exception of the elaborate headquarters of the Austrian secret service. Almost the only exterior is a few feet of snow-covered ground outside the inn, and a rainy street in an Austrian town.

Picture No. 9 is laid in France—the earlier scenes in Paris and the later ones in the country. We are given some good although not extensive views of a Parisian boulevard, and also of a small French railway station. There are, however, practically no scenes of the French countryside.

Picture No. 10 is not a very good example of foreign locale, since only the last scene is laid abroad, and that in a French sidewalk café.

The opening scenes of Picture No. 11 take place in a rather indefinite country, presumably somewhere in the Balkans, but here we see little besides the Duke's castle. The rest of the picture is laid in Monte Carlo, and there is one effective shot of the resort by daylight, and another by night, showing a glittering chain of lights beside the sea. The rest of the action is confined to interiors.

In Picture No. 12 we are given a splendid presentation of Morocco. The shots are not only, many of them, scenically beautiful, but quite varied, including the desert, the native quarters, the streets, markets, minarets, and cafés. Here again the effects achieved are very real.

Picture No. 13 is another which gives an excellent portrayal of its locale, Sumatra, where the story was actually filmed.

Picture No. 14 is placed in Russia. There are views of a Russian village, a snowy mountain pass, a market place in the city, and a number of scenes of a native tribe moving across the country to another location. There are also some picturesque scenes near a little lake and on the estate surrounding the castle of the heroine's uncle.

Only a few scenes of Picture No. 15 are laid in Mexico, and here we see nothing except the interior of a combined gambling den and café.

Much of the action of Picture No. 16 is laid abroad, but the scenes are not given in great detail. There is one background of Mexican countryside, showing peons working, and the action then shifts to the courtyard and interior of a small Mexican inn. There is a glimpse of a casino, presumably at Monte Carlo; a wealthy Spanish home, all interior scenes except a terrace and a gateway; a hotel and an office in Paris; the interior of a ballroom, ostensibly in London.

Picture No. 17 is laid entirely in England, with the exception of one scene in a village in the mountains of France. This is perhaps more typical than the English scenes, where we see little except interiors. There is one incident, however, where the hero and heroine take a bus ride in London, but we get only passing glimpses of street scenes and no views of the show spots of this city.

Two reviewers familiar with these 17 feature pictures classified the depiction of foreign locales as follows: 4, excellent; 2, good; 5, fair; 6, poor.

SETTINGS

Do the locales placed in the United States give the observer a sympathetic, discriminating, and representative insight as to the settings in which the drama of American and foreign life unfolds? What are the settings in which the action of the characters of the photoplay takes place?

TABLE 7

EXTERIOR SETTINGS SEEN IN 7 OR MORE OF THE 115 PICTURES

Number and per cent of pictures in which each type of exterior was shown

Type of Exterior	Number	Per cent
Street	40	35
House	26	23
Deck of ship	22	19
Garden	22	19
Road	18	16
Western country	10	9
Beach	9	8
Village	9	8
Hotel	8	7
Ocean	8	7
Veranda—Porch	8	7
Café	7	6
Courtyard	7	6
Lawn or yard	7	6
Outdoors (General)	7	6
Theater	7	6
Town	7	6
Train	7	6

Exterior Settings

Tables 7 and 8 indicate in order of frequency the exterior settings in 115 motion pictures. The most frequently used exterior settings are as follows: A street appears in 35 per cent of the pictures, and the exterior view of a house provides a background for action in 23 per cent. Next in rank is the deck of a ship, with 19 per cent of the pictures; a garden is also used in 19 per cent; and a road in 16 per cent.

TABLE 8

EXTERIOR SETTINGS SEEN IN LESS THAN 7 OF THE 115 PICTURES

Number of pictures in which each type of exterior was shown

Type of Exterior	Number	Type of Exterior	Number
Apartment house	6	Lake shore and scene	2
Castle—Palace	6	Market	2
City	6	Prison camp	2
Flying field	6	Roof garden	2
Park	6	Rooming house	2
Stadium	6	Schoolyard	2
Store—Shop	6	Sidewalk	2
Camp	5	Stagecoach	2
Dock—Pier	5	Stockade	2
In air	5	Woods	2
Jungle	5	Alley	1
Night club—Cabaret	5	Amusement park	1
Office building	5	Antarctic regions	1
River bank	5	Army post	1
Saloon	5	Bank	1
Terrace	5	Barracks	1
Football field	4	Bazaar	1
Ranch	4	Bottom of sea	1
Seacoast	4	Broadcasting station	1
Station platform	4	Château	1
Airport	3	College building	1
Balcony	3	Crossroads	1
Cabin	3	Explorer's camp	1
Country	3	Farm	1
Country club	3	Golf course	1
Desert	3	Graveyard	1
Hut	3	Harbor	1
Mountains	3	Hospital	1
Patio	3	Inn	1
Plains	3	Island	1
Polo field	3	Lakehurst Naval Station	1
Prison	3	North woods	1
Street corner	3	On top of bus	1
Army encampment	2	Orphanage	1
Battlefield	2	Parade ground	1
Campus	2	Path	1
Casino	2	Penthouse roof	1
Church—Cathedral	2	Police station	1
Cottage	2	Prison courtyard	1
Depot	2	Roadside stand	1
Fair	2	Sidewalk café	1
Forest	2	Slaughterhouse	1
Grandstand	2	Tabernacle	1
Hangar	2	Tournament field	1
Jail	2		

TABLE 9

INDUSTRIAL AND COMMERCIAL SETTINGS SEEN IN THE 115 PICTURES

Number and per cent of pictures in which each setting was shown

Type of Exterior	No.	Per cent	Type of Interior	No.	Per cent
Store—Shop........	6	5	Office............	40	35
Office building.......	5	4	Workshop—Lab-	4	3
Market.............	2	2	oratory......	3	3
Bank..............	1	1	Bank............	3	3
Bazaar.............	1	1	Beauty parlor—		
Roadside stand......	1	1	Barber shop..	3	3
Slaughter house......	1	1	Store—Shop......	3	3
			Factory..........	1	1
			Newspaper office		
			City room......	1	1
			Press room.....	1	1
			Press box........	1	1
			Warehouse.......	1	1

The exterior settings which occur in less than 7 pictures are listed in Table 8. Table 9 shows the number and per cent of exteriors and interiors devoted to portraying industrial and commercial activities. One can conclude that opportunity for visual acquaintanceship with commerce and industry, as indicated by these sets, is quite meager.

It is evident from a study of these tables that the motion picture does give to the viewer a wide variety of experiences with different settings. Perhaps its major weakness is a failure to give us an adequate conception of industry and agriculture. The failure to include scenes such as these may be due to the fact that critical problems of agriculture and industry have as yet received scant attention in the motion pictures. Further, the movie makers apparently have not fully realized the interest-heightening value of short glimpses into the workaday world. We need more scenes like the cotton gin and the sawmill in "Hallelujah," the bank vault in "American Madness," the skyscraper scenes in "Fast Workers," the farm scenes in "State Fair."

TABLE 10

INTERIOR SETTINGS SEEN IN 5 OR MORE OF THE 115 PICTURES
Number and per cent of pictures in which each type of interior was shown

Type of Interior	Number	Per cent
Bedroom	49	43
Living room	45	39
Office	40	35
Hall	25	22
Interior (General)	23	20
Dining—Breakfast room	21	18
Hotel—Inn, Room—Suite	20	17
Kitchen	20	17
Drawing room	16	14
Theater, Stage	15	13
Aboard train	14	12
Room	14	12
Sitting room—Parlor	13	11
Library	12	10
Night club—Cabaret	12	10
Café	11	10
Prison cell	11	10
Aboard ship, Stateroom—Cabin	10	9
Boudoir	10	9
Hospital	10	9
Hotel, Lobby	10	9
Saloon	10	9
Theater, Dressing room	10	9
Auditorium	9	8
Automobile	9	8
Ballroom	9	8
Church—Cathedral	8	7
Hut	8	7
Restaurant—Cafeteria	8	7
Anteroom	7	6
Bathroom—Shower room	7	6
Ranch—Farmhouse	7	6
Club	6	5
Den—Study	6	5
Jail—Prison	6	5
Night club—Cabaret, Dressing room	6	5
Courtroom	5	3
Gambling house	5	3
Studio	5	3
Telephone booth	5	3
Tent	5	3

Interior Settings

Table 10 shows the most frequently used interior settings, many of which are rooms in residences. The most popular interior set is the bedroom, which appears in 43 per cent of the pictures. The extremely high frequency of the bedroom as a setting is probably explainable on two bases. First of all, it is an important room in the home. Second, it is evident that it is used to heighten the expectation of the audience. For example, Elmer Rice says:

> The mere presence upon the stage of a bed never fails to provoke an audience to a state of expectancy, despite the fact that the sight of this article of furniture is a commonplace in everyone's daily life.[1]

The living room is used in 39 per cent of the pictures. Third in rank is an office, used in 35 per cent of the pictures.

The fact that 10 per cent of the motion pictures used a library as an interior set also seems significant. Interestingly enough, however, in none of the 4 pictures (of the 40 analyzed in detail) in which there was a library, was a character shown reading a book.

The combining of the settings of *theater and stage* and *night club—cabaret* produces a large number of settings. This high proportion is doubtless due to the opportunity thus afforded for the display of dancing, singing, or other musical activities.

An examination of Table 11, which includes the interiors found in less than 7 of the pictures, is illuminating. Certainly, through the motion picture the child and the adult are given a series of interesting glimpses into homes, dwelling places, and places of business, admittance to which they are ordinarily denied.

[1] "Sex in the Modern Theater," *Harper's Magazine*, 164 (May 1932), pp. 665–673.

TABLE 11

Number of pictures in which each type of interior was shown

Type of Interior	Number	Type of Interior	Number
Cabin	4	Nursery	2
Classroom—Schoolroom	4	Rest room	2
Depot	4	Tenement	2
Hotel—Inn	4	Aboard elevated train	1
Taxi	4	Aboard ship	
Theater		Brig	1
Backstage—Wings	4	Captain's office	1
Lobby	4	Deck	1
Workshop—Laboratory	4	Engine room	1
Aboard ship, Wireless room	3	Hospital	1
Aboard subway car	3	Kitchen	1
Assembly hall	3	Pilot house	1
Bank	3	Aboard street car	1
Banquet hall	3	Art gallery	1
Barn	3	Cave	1
Beauty parlor—Barber		College chapel	1
shop	3	Factory	1
Broadcasting studio	3	Flower show	1
Casino	3	Hack	1
Garage	3	Hotel, Dining room	1
Lobby	3	Institution	
Locker room—Dressing		Dining room	1
room	3	Hall	1
Military headquarters	3	Nursery	1
Police station	3	Parlor	1
Speakeasy	3	Room—Suite	1
Store—Shop	3	Legislative chamber	1
Aboard airplane	2	Newspaper office	
Aboard dirigible	2	City room	1
Aboard ship		Press room	1
Corridor	2	Pavilion	1
Salon	2	Pool room	1
Swimming pool	2	Press box	1
Barracks	2	Public library	1
Billiard room	2	Red Cross Station	1
Building	2	Servants' quarters	1
Cellar—Basement	2	Stagecoach	1
Dance hall	2	Tabernacle	1
Gymnasium	2	Theater, Property room	1
Hotel, Ballroom	2	Torture chamber	1
Hangar	2	Tunnel	1
Institution, Dormitory	2	Warehouse	1
Madison Square Garden	2		

Economic Status of Residences

Table 12 indicates the economic levels [2] of the residences in which the characters lived. Twenty-two per cent of the residences were ultra-wealthy; 47 per cent were

TABLE 12

ECONOMIC STATUS OF THE RESIDENCES IN THE 40 PICTURES

Number and per cent of settings and of pictures in which residences of each status were shown

Status	Settings		Pictures	
	Number	Per cent	Number	Per cent
Ultra-wealthy	50	22	9	23
Wealthy	108	47	21	53
Moderate	58	25	17	43
Poor	9	4	5	13
Indeterminate	3	1	3	8
Total	228	100		

TABLE 13

TYPE OF RESIDENCE SEEN IN THE 40 PICTURES

Number and per cent of settings and of pictures in which each type of residence is used

Type	Settings		Pictures	
	Number	Per cent	Number	Per cent
House	116	51	24	60
Apartment	67	29	15	38
Castle—Palace	13	6	3	8
Rooming house	10	4	5	13
General	22	10	12	30
Total	228	100		

wealthy; 25 per cent, moderate; 4 per cent, definitely poor; and 1 per cent, indeterminate. When we combine the ultra-wealthy and the wealthy groups, we include 69 per cent of

[2] See Chapter IV, pp. 47–48, for an explanation of these 4 categories.

all residences, almost three times as many as the moderate group. The types of residence in which the characters live are indicated in Table 13.

These data, in conjunction with those relating to interiors, lead to certain interesting speculations. What values are likely to come from displaying to children and adults scenes of homes most of which are far above the economic level of the viewer? It is clear that many such persons will have their taste improved by scenes which they see. However, much of what is seen in the decoration and the interiors of homes of wealth is inapplicable in the homes of the viewers of motion pictures. For example, we see only rarely in the motion-picture settings an emphasis on good taste as displayed in the homes of persons of meager income.

The final effect, therefore, of such settings upon the immature or even the mature individual is not easily determined. The conclusion seems inescapable, however, that not infrequently envy and dissatisfaction are likely to follow the consistent and extravagant display of wealth in the motion pictures. Energy that might be used for thoughtful planning as to methods of attaining one's ideals may be dissipated in day-dreaming and fanciful thinking about unattainable goals. Dewey says on this point in *Human Nature and Conduct:*

> The evils of idle dreaming and of routine are experienced in conjunction. "Idealism" must indeed come first—the imagination of some better state generated by desire. But unless ideals are to be dreams and idealism a synonym for romanticism and phantasy-building, there must be a most realistic study of actual conditions and of the mode or law of natural events, in order to give the imagined or ideal object definite form and solid substance—to give it, in short, practicality and constitute it a working end.[3]

[3] Dewey, John, *Human Nature and Conduct,* New York: Henry Holt and Company, 1922, p. 236.

The movie setting as it relates to interiors very clearly does not offer us a "realistic study of actual conditions."

SUMMARY

The study of the settings and locales was based on the 115 pictures which were actually viewed and on the 40 of these which were studied in greater detail. Over half the pictures were set entirely in the United States, while about one fifth were entirely foreign. The remaining were indeterminate or some combination of the three classifications. The most frequent specific locale was New York City which was seen in 19 per cent of the pictures. Next to the United States, France was seen most often, followed by England. The next most common locale was "a ship at sea." Metropolitan locales were stressed. They accounted for 38 per cent of all locales, 52 per cent of all United States locales, and 28 per cent of all foreign locales. The detailed description of the foreign scenes leaves one with the impression that the view of foreign countries, while excellent at points, was in general inadequate.

Locales were then analyzed to greater depth and critical data were secured concerning interior and exterior settings. Interior settings were seen slightly more often than exteriors. One hundred and seven different types of exteriors were shown. Two of these were shown in one fifth or more of the pictures. One hundred and nineteen types of interiors were shown, five of which were shown in one fifth or more of the pictures. None of the exterior scenes was seen as often as either of the two first interiors, which were *bedroom* and *living room*. *Office* ranked third, being shown in the same number of pictures as a *street*, the first in rank for exteriors.

The residences are usually houses, though a significant proportion consists of apartments. They are decidedly in the upper economic strata; 69 per cent being ultra-wealthy or wealthy, 25 per cent moderate, and but 4 per cent poor.

In the matter of economic status there has been, in the opinion of the writer, an overemphasis on the ultra-wealthy and wealthy classes. The effect of such portrayals on certain members of the audience has been shown by Dr. Blumer's studies. Such portrayal should be included if life is to be truthfully presented, but the emphasis now being placed upon these classes is entirely unjustified in terms of truthful presentation of life.

CHAPTER IV

WHAT ARE THE MOVIE CHARACTERS LIKE?

WHO are the characters who every week delight and thrill that vast audience which in 1929 was estimated to contain 11,000,000 children, 17,000,000 youth, and 49,000,000 adults? Are these characters young or old, rich or poor? Do they work for a living, or do they live off the labor of others? Do they make their living honestly or dishonestly? And what is the specific nature of their occupation? Do they closely resemble the members of the vast audience who view them, or are they remote from them in interest and experience?

These and other questions of a similar nature demand an answer. There is little doubt of the tremendous public admiration of movie stars, and this admiration may extend in some degree to the rôles which they portray. If, then, these rôles are those which can be approved by parents and others interested in the character development of their children, the movies may be doing a tremendous amount of good. Conversely, if the leading characters play attractive rôles which are socially disapproved, a vast amount of harm may be done those who view the picture.

The nature of the content of motion pictures is also indicated in some degree by the characteristics of the leading characters. If they are primarily people in their twenties, we may well expect that the motion picture will to a great extent deal with the activities of young folk. If, on the other hand, we find that middle-aged characters figure prominently on the screen, then we shall discover problems faced by persons at this age level.

The Ages of Leading Characters

The ages of the leading characters were obtained for only 40 pictures. The age has been estimated, and two observers, working independently, agree very closely in their estimates. The divergence is greatest in the case of characters beyond

TABLE 14

Ages of Leading Characters in the 40 Pictures

Number and per cent of each type of leading character in each age group

Age Group a	Type of Character												Total	
	Hero b		Heroine b		Villain c		Vil-lainess c		Other Men		Other Women			
	No.	Per cent	No.	Per cent	No.	Per cent	No.	Per cent	No.	Per cent	No.	Per cent	No.	Per cent
1–5									1		1		1	
6–13			1	3					12	7	1	2	14	4
14–18	1	3	2	5			1	14	3	2	3	6	10	3
19–22	3	8	11	28					11	6	11	20	36	10
23–26	4	10	22	56			2	29	12	7	8	15	48	14
27–30	20	51	2	5	3	10	2	29	16	9	5	9	48	14
31–35	7	18	1	3	9	30	1	14	29	16	4	7	51	15
36–40	2	5			9	30			26	15	9	17	46	13
41–45					5	17			12	7	1	2	18	5
46–50									21	12	7	13	28	8
51–55	2	5			3	10			17	10	4	7	26	8
56–60							1	14	15	9	1	2	17	5
61–70					1	3							1	
71–80														
81–90														
Total	39	100	39	100	30	100	7	100	175	100	54	100	344	100

a Logical age grouping, rather than equal intervals, is used.

b These terms are used to designate the attractive leading male and female characters.

c These terms are used to designate the unsympathized-with leading male and female characters.

the age of 45. The essential data secured by this analysis of the ages of leading characters is presented in Table 14.

The reader will note that 56 per cent, or 22 heroines, are between the ages of 23 and 26—a striking majority of the total number of heroines. Further, 28 per cent, or 11, of the heroines were between the ages of 19 and 22. If we add these two figures together, we discover that 84 per cent of the heroines in these 40 pictures were between the ages of 19 and 26.

The heroes, however, are older. Fifty-one per cent are between the ages of 27 and 30. Next in number is the age group between 31 and 35, which includes 18 per cent. We see, therefore, that 69 per cent of the heroes are between the ages of 27 and 35.

What about the villains? We see at once that they are older than the heroes, since the age group from 31 to 40 includes 60 per cent of the villains. Only 10 per cent of them are between the ages of 27 and 30. No villains are under 27, although 21 per cent of the heroes are under this age.

The villainesses, interestingly enough, are young women, only 28 per cent of them being above 31 years of age. The numbers here, of course, are very small and generalizations are hazardous.

The other leading characters who appeared in the pictures tend to be older than the heroes and heroines. It will be noted that 69 per cent of the 175 men are 31 years of age or over.

The evidence here presented demonstrates clearly that motion pictures are built around the activities of young men and women, and only secondarily include as their major activities the portrayal of events in the lives of older persons or children. This is strikingly brought out, for example, by the fact that only two of the 39 heroes are from 51 to 55 years of age, and there is not one hero in the age group from 41 to 50. Further, no heroine is older than 35.

What do these data mean? Is it possible that the most dramatic conflicts in life occur between the ages of 20 and 30? The writer would venture the hypothesis that these data represent the belief on the part of the motion-picture producers that the majority of their audience is young. Strikingly enough, there are few data published on the ages of the motion-picture habitués except those published in a companion study by the writer. Although this study does not indicate the per cent of the audience at the different age levels above 21, it points out that almost two thirds of the audience is adult.

When we consider, however, that 37 per cent of the population is 35 years of age or over (1930 census), we soon discover that there is a potential audience of huge size to which the producers are not catering. The producers may reply, of course, that they are catering to the younger members of their audience, and that what this group wants to see is not middle-aged romance or the problems of middle-aged persons but youthful romance.

However, when the *Motion Picture Herald* canvassed theaters in the leading cities to determine the most profitable pictures of 1932, "Emma," in which Marie Dressler starred, was one of the group, as was "The Man Who Played God," in which George Arliss starred. "Emma" has almost no love story at all in it. There is, however, a love story in "The Man Who Played God." But, judging by personal appearance, the leading character in each of these pictures is well past 60.

ECONOMIC STATUS OF LEADING CHARACTERS

A common criticism of motion pictures is that their leading characters are too largely recruited from the wealthier classes, and further, that they concern themselves far more with the problems and activities of the upper vocational or professional levels than they do with the problems of the laboring class. There is a feeling that this alleged preoccupation with the wealthy, professional, or leisure group breeds envy and imitation among the less favored or results in a vicious type of wishful thinking. The writer is not here concerned with the effects of the alleged emphasis on the upper class activities but presents the facts as discovered in the study of the occupational and economic level of the leading characters in the 115 motion pictures which were analyzed.

Table 15 presents the data on the economic status of 811 leading characters found in 115 pictures.

TABLE 15

ECONOMIC STATUS OF LEADING CHARACTERS IN THE 115 PICTURES

Number and per cent of each type of character in each economic group

Economic Status	Character												Total	
	Hero		Heroine		Villain		Villainess		Other Men		Other Women			
	No.	Per cent	No.	Per cent	No.	Per cent	No.	Per cent	No.	Per cent	No.	Per cent	No.	Per cent
Ultra-wealthy	10	9	8	7	5	7	3	16	17	5	9	6	52	6
Wealthy..	28	24	44	37	35	47	9	47	88	26	46	33	250	31
Moderate.	64	55	52	44	26	35	6	32	181	53	57	40	386	48
Poor.....	13	11	15	13	4	5	1	5	44	13	21	15	98	12
Indeterminate...	1	1			5	7			11	3	8	6	25	3
Total.....	116	100	119	100	75	100	19	100	341	100	141	100	811	100

These characters have been classed under four groups: ultra-wealthy, wealthy, in moderate circumstances, and poor. A character is ultra-wealthy when he and his surroundings show evidences of unusual wealth. The wealth is evidenced by a number of servants, including probably either a valet or a personal maid; an immense house, more elaborately decorated and furnished than the home ordinarily considered wealthy. A character is considered wealthy when the circumstances under which he lives suggest an income considerably above that received by persons in moderate circumstances. The moderate category includes persons in comfortable circumstances, members of the middle class, those characters whose lives appear to be free from undue financial care. A person is considered poor only when there are external evidences of poverty such as ragged clothing, insufficient food, and so on.

If will be noted in Table 15 that the number of both heroes and heroines exceeds the total number of pictures. This is due to the fact that the economic status of a character sometimes changes in a picture, and we have tabulated them twice when this has occurred.

From this table we see at once that motion pictures concern themselves in far greater degree with ultra-wealthy and wealthy leading characters than the proportion of these to be found in the general population would justify. Nine per cent of the heroes are ultra-wealthy and 24 per cent are wealthy. Thirty-three per cent, therefore, are either wealthy or ultra-wealthy. Seven per cent of the heroines are ultra-wealthy, 37 per cent are wealthy. Fifty-four per cent are either wealthy or ultra-wealthy. Fifty-four per cent of the villains are either wealthy or ultra-wealthy, and 63 per cent of the villainesses are either wealthy or ultra-wealthy.

Further, there are as many heroines in the wealthy and ultra-wealthy groups combined as there are in the "moderate circumstances" group, 44 per cent. Fifty-four per cent of the villains are found in both the ultra-wealthy and wealthy categories but only 35 per cent are in moderate circumstances.

Only 32 per cent of the villainesses are in moderate circumstances, as opposed to 63 per cent who are in either the wealthy or the ultra-wealthy category. The leading characters who are "poor" range from villains and villainesses with 5 per cent each to 15 per cent for the other leading women characters.

We note that the number of villains and villainesses who are wealthy or ultra-wealthy exceeds the number of the heroes and heroines in these classes. Further, poor leading characters are rarely shown as villains and villainesses.

Preoccupation with the more favored social groups is evidenced here, as was also discovered in the data on settings. Defense of this procedure will probably run along these lines: When one attends the theater he is seeking release from actuality. Therefore, since the majority of the population has only a meager income and lives fairly close to the subsistence level, we may expect that they will want their movies to portray not people like themselves, but rather people in greatly different economic and social status. Through the movies the audience is able to explore vicariously the activities and emotions of the favored classes, the economically and socially privileged.

This view of the function of the drama is one with which the writer is not in accord. While he believes that there are times when the patient is suffering so much that he needs a drug, he believes that this prescription has been overdone. He believes with Wells that: (Substitute for the word "novel" the words "motion picture.")

> You see now the scope of the claim I am making for the novel: it is to be the social mediator, the vehicle of understanding, the instrument of self-examination, the parade of morals and the exchange of manners, the factory of customs and ideas, the criticism of laws and institutions and of social dogmas and ideas. It is to be the home confessional, the initiator of knowledge, the seed of fruitful self-questioning. Let me be very clear here, I do not mean for a moment that the novelist is going to set up as a teacher, as a sort of priest, with a pen, who will make men and women believe and do this and that. The novel is not a new sort of pulpit. . . . But the novelist is going to present con-

duct, devise beautiful conduct, discuss conduct, analyze conduct, suggest conduct, illuminate it through and through. . . .

We are going to write, subject only to our own limitations, about the whole of human life. We are going to deal with political questions and religious questions and social questions. We cannot present people unless we have this free hand, this unrestricted field. . . .

We are going to write about it all . . . until a thousand pretenses and ten thousand impostures shrivel in the cold, clear air of our elucidations. We are going to write of wasted opportunities and latent beauties, until a thousand new ways of living open to men and women.[1]

OCCUPATIONS OF LEADING CHARACTERS

What sort of glimpse into the workaday world does the motion picture give us? Does it show:

"Hog Butcher for the World,
Tool Maker, Stacker of Wheat,
Player with Railroads and the Nation's Freight Handler;
Stormy, husky, brawling,
City of the Big Shoulders:

.   .   .   .

     Bareheaded,
     Shoveling,
     Wrecking,
     Planning,
     Building, breaking, rebuilding, . . ."[2]

Does the modern movie show the manual or professional worker in the context of a world fabric? Is the concept of interdependence sympathetically and dramatically presented? Do we see a prophetic hope of a society in which orders shall not filter down from above, but in which the intelligence of all is given a chance to direct operations?

A study of Table 16 will show that our hopes for such

[1] Wells, H. G., "The Contemporary Novel," *Atlantic Monthly*, CIX (January 1912), pp. 6, 10–11.
[2] Sandburg, Carl, "Chicago," *Chicago Poems*, New York: Henry Holt and Company, 1916, p. 3.

clarification of social contributions through one's work are unjustified. The most striking fact of all is that "no occupation" seems to be the lot of the majority of leading characters. However, one should note that only eight of the 583 leading male characters have no occupation, while 124 of the 300 leading female characters enjoy this distinction. An additional survey revealed that approximately 50 per cent of the women having no occupation were married.

The dominance of *commercial occupations* is striking. No less important, however, is the fact that *illegal occupation* ranks third. Under *illegal occupation* we have placed such activities as gangster, bootlegger, smuggler, thief, prostitute, bandit, and blackmailer.

If we consider each type of character separately, we see that *illegal occupation* is fourth in rank for heroes, fifth in rank for the heroines (although it divides this rank with three other occupations), highest in rank for the villains, third in rank for the villainesses. For other men it shares fourth rank with professional men, and for other women it ranks sixth. Had only leading characters been considered under *servants*, however, these ranks would probably have been third and fifth respectively. In total ranking, *occupation unknown* shares third rank with *illegal occupation*. The following distinction is drawn between *no occupation* and *occupation unknown:* If a character is definitely shown as doing nothing useful or not earning a living, he is placed in the *no occupation* category; but if he seemingly has an occupation, although it is impossible to determine from the picture exactly what it is that he does, he is listed under *occupation unknown*.

The recruitment of leading characters from the theatrical profession is evidenced by the rank of *theatrical* among the leading occupations. It ranks seventh for the heroes

109/13

TABLE 16

OCCUPATIONS OF LEADING CHARACTERS IN THE 115 PICTURES

Number of each type of character in each occupation

Occupation	Type of Character						Total
	Hero	Heroine	Villain	Villainess	Other Men	Other Women	
1. No occupation [a]	2	54	1	6	5	64	132
2. Commercial	14	10	7	1	45	13	90
3. Illegal occupation	11	5	22	3	31	8	80
4. Occupation unknown	19	5	13	1	39	3	80
5. Theatrical	6	21	8	2	23	16	76
6. Servants	5	4	1		43 [b]	15 [b]	68
7. Professional	23	3	3	1	31	3	64
8. "High society"	8	9	8	4	11	10	50
9. Military	8	2	7	1	22	1	41
10. Academic	3	5	2	2	16	7	35
11. Public service	5		1		22		28
12. Personal service	2	5			9	4	20
13. Agricultural	6	2	1		9	1	19
14. Children	1	1			14	1	17
15. Naval	6		1		8		15
16. Miscellaneous	1	2	1		7	1	12
17. Merchant marine	4		2	1	3		10
18. Prison	4		3		3		10
19. Aviation	1		1		7		9
20. Religious		1			7	1	9
21. Scientific	1		1		5		7
22. Transportation	2	1	1		3		7
23. Marines	1				1		2
24. Common labor			1				1
25. Retired					1		1
Total	133	130	85	22	365	148	883

[a] An additional survey revealed that approximately 50 per cent of the women having no occupation were married.
[b] All servants, not just the leading characters, were included here.

(sharing this rank with two others), second for the heroines, and third for the villains (sharing this rank with one other). The reasons for such a high percentage of leading characters in this rôle are perhaps many. Most significant, however, is the fact that by having members of the theatrical profession in leading rôles, it becomes possible to present musical and other entertainment as legitimate parts of the motion picture.

It is significant that the occupation of the highest percentage of heroes is *professional*. Perhaps in this fact we get some clues as to the tremendous gaps in prestige between what may be termed vocations and the professions. The term *professional* here is interpreted as including the so-called professions, *i.e.*, law and medicine (but not the ministry, which is presented under *religious*, nor teaching, which is included under *academic*), and in addition literary, artistic, political, and engineering occupations.

The classification *high society* is a special one, not exactly parallel to the others presented. It was set up in an attempt to discover whether the occupations of the leading characters consisted of "society" activities. The fact that this category ranks eighth [3] in total occupations shows that *high society* is the preoccupation of a significant proportion of the leading characters.

In the total column *military* ranks ninth, *naval* fifteenth, and *marines* twenty-third. Combined, they would rank eighth. *Agriculture* ranks thirteenth, but this rank is due almost entirely to the inclusion of Western pictures dealing with ranching.

Certainly, according to the present movie fare, we shall not expect to see portrayed there the problems of land tenancy, the changing mores of agricultural communities,

[3] All ranks above 6 for the total group, above 2 for *other men*, and 3 for *other women* may be one rank too high due to the inclusion of all servants and not just leading characters under that category.

the fading of pioneer psychology, and so on. Science, transportation, common labor, get short shrift at the hands of the movie makers. Only rarely will we get a glimpse on the screen of those intrepid workers, such as Koch, Pasteur, Grenfell, Steinmetz, and others who through their scientific investigations have profoundly modified the world in which we live.

The Depiction of Foreigners and Less-Favored Races

One common objective in materials on history and the social sciences is to develop a friendly understanding of foreign races. Such instruction may begin as early as the first grade, where children read stories about children of many lands, the Dutch, Chinese, Japanese, Eskimos, and many others. In a progressive high school it may involve units of study dealing with foreign groups within the city, their racial histories, their difficulties, and how they have solved them. The breaking down of racial prejudice and the setting up of intelligent attitudes toward persons of other races is therefore a fundamental objective in intelligent secular and religious education. Wise parents coöperate with the school and the church in furthering such objectives.

And then these children go to the movies. If they live in cities where theaters are accessible, children over the age of seven will average one attendance a week. What do they see there? Does the feature motion picture emphasize the idea that many Chinese are noble and kindly? Are Mexicans frequently shown as kindly and friendly? Are Negroes often shown in a favorable light? Or do we find verifications here for a number of the accusations made in Bruno Lasker's study, *Race Attitudes in Children*? He says:

> Movies show foreigners and Negroes as comic characters or to their disadvantage, writes a settlement worker.

The New Jersey group of parents, repeatedly quoted in this book, report: The group considered that in regard to strength and permanency of influence the strongest factor today is to be found in the motion picture where much race discrimination is subtly taught.

A middle-western teacher writes: Movies will use villains who are Mexicans or Italians, or just look foreign. But I feel there is less of this now than there was formerly.[4]

In this same book we find the following:

A correspondent gives a concrete example of international prejudice induced by a film. It occurred in Raleigh, N. C., last month. The film is called "Foreign Devils," and the story is based on the Boxer uprising in China in 1900. It was shown on Saturday night. Next day a teacher in a Sunday School was explaining to a class that children of all countries are children of a common Father. One child responded, "I saw a movie last night, and the Chinese are terrible people."

Another observer writes:

Foreigners and traveled persons see the need for more information in the making of scenes of foreign countries and foreign peoples. The idea of ridiculing other nationalities and showing only their faults is very irritating. It not only creates a bitter feeling abroad but also becomes partly responsible for the erroneous idea that the average American has of the rest of the world.[5]

One way in which prejudice may be shown is through using the characters as clowns or buffoons. While some might object to classifying this as a form of race prejudice, nevertheless none of us would like to have our own race constantly presented in this light. It is also possible to show the character in a definitely unattractive light. Personal

[4] Lasker, Bruno, *Race Attitudes in Children*, New York: Henry Holt and Company, 1929, p. 200.
[5] *Ibid.*, p. 200.

TABLE 17

Depiction of Nationalities as Humorous, Attractive, or Unattractive in the 40 Pictures

Number of persons of each nationality represented in each group

Nationality	Humorous			Non-Humorous									Total		
				Attractive			Unattractive			Total					
	Men	Women	Both	Men	Women	Both	Men	Women	Both	Men	Women	Both	Men	Women	Both
French.......	7	2	9	5	4	9	2	....	2	7	4	11	14	6	20
English......	4	2	6	2	2	4	2	2	4	4	4	8	8	6	14
Russian......	1	....	1	4	4	8	2	1	3	6	5	11	7	5	12
Am. Negro...	3	2	5	1	....	1	....	....	....	1	....	1	4	2	6
Swedish......	5	....	5	....	....	....	....	1	1	....	1	1	5	1	6
Jewish.......	3	1	4	1	....	1	....	....	....	1	....	1	4	1	5
German......	1	....	1	2	....	2	2	....	2	4	....	4	5	....	5
Moroccan....	....	1	1	....	2	2	....	2	2	2	2	4	2	3	5
Am. Indian...	2	1	3	....	....	....	1	....	1	1	....	1	3	1	4
Austrian.....	1	....	1	2	1	3	....	....	....	2	1	3	3	1	4
Italian.......	3	....	3	....	....	....	....	....	....	....	....	....	3	....	3
Irish.........	1	1	2	1	....	1	....	....	....	1	....	1	2	1	3
Spanish......	1	1	2	....	....	....	....	....	....	....	....	....	1	1	2
Mexican.....	....	1	1	....	....	....	....	1	1	....	1	1	....	2	2
Sumatran....	....	....	....	2	....	2	....	....	....	2	....	2	2	....	2
Japanese.....	2	....	2	....	....	....	....	....	....	....	....	....	2	....	2
Chinese......	1	....	1	....	....	....	....	....	....	....	....	....	1	....	1
Scotch.......	1	....	1	....	....	....	....	....	....	....	....	....	1	....	1
Hungarian...	....	....	....	....	1	1	....	....	....	....	1	1	....	1	1
Portuguese...	1	....	1	....	....	....	....	....	....	....	....	....	1	....	1
Turkish......	1	....	1	....	....	....	....	....	....	....	....	....	1	....	1
Cuban.......	....	....	....	....	....	....	1	....	1	1	....	1	1	....	1
Hawaiian....	....	....	....	....	1	1	....	....	....	....	1	1	....	1	1
Total........	38	12	50	20	15	35	12	5	17	32	20	52	70	32	102

appearance and actions, *e.g.*, vicious, crafty, dirty, sissified, simpering, excitable, impetuous, are factors in this unattractiveness.

What are the facts as discovered in our analysis? Table 17 presents the depiction of foreigners and underprivileged races in the 40 pictures which we studied in detail. It is read as follows: Seven French men and 2 French women were shown as humorous characters, making a total of 9.

Five French men and 4 French women were shown as attractive, but non-humorous, making a total of 9. Two French men and no French women were shown as unattractive, making a total of 2 unattractive French characters. There is a total of 7 men and 4 women, making 11 in all, who are shown as non-humorous characters. Further, the total of all French characters in the 40 pictures constitutes 14 men and 6 women, 20 in all. The descriptions of the French characters follow:

Paul, a barber by profession, is a large plump man with a little black mustache, the mincing type of Frenchman, immaculately dressed in the latest style.

The mayor is a large, fat-faced Frenchman with mutton-chop whiskers, who sleeps at every opportunity, speaks very bad English and nasal French.

Felice, who speaks with a slight French accent, is wearing a simple print dress with a long full skirt, and her shoulder-length, curly blonde hair is tied back with a ribbon.

Fleurette, who has black eyes and straight black hair, bobbed and cut with bangs, is dressed in a black and white suit, carries a white poodle tucked under arm, and speaks with a French accent.

Leonie, a penniless member of the French aristocracy, is young and beautiful, but there is nothing distinctively French in either her appearance or her speech.

Armand, the hero's friend, is a short, dark Frenchman, well-dressed, and with but a trace of accent.

The captain's daughter, whose father is French and mother is American, is just an ordinarily pretty girl who speaks French and also speaks English without an accent.

Armande is short and brunet, handsome, and evidences his race in little except what the audience is informed is a decided Gascon accent.

The Frenchman occupying the same train compartment as the heroine is an offensive appearing individual with a monocle and a lisp.

The chief officer, Crosetti, is an excitable man who is always shouting in broken English.

The High Commissioner of the Republic is a pompous, elderly man in a frock coat and high silk hat, who looks about in a displeased fashion and grumbles because he is not paid the proper respect.

Louise, a French countess, is a woman of about thirty-five, whose clothing follows the style of seventeenth century France, but whose visible French characteristics cease with that point.

The heroine's husband is a dark-complexioned Frenchman of medium height, who has very little accent, but is depicted as excitable and suspicious of his wife.

An elderly well-dressed Frenchman in a sidewalk café holds up his glass and drinks to the health of the hero and heroine.

Among the passengers on the boat is a Frenchman of about forty-five, dark, wearing a little black mustache, and very well-dressed.

Their guide is a very shabby Frenchman, who shuffles along before them, and alternates between rapid French and very bad English.

Napoleon appears, a small, careworn man in a tight-fitting uniform and a tricorne, who speaks in a ringing voice without a trace of accent.

De Grignon, a French Royalist, is an elaborately uniformed, rather simpering dandy, whose speech is without a French accent.

The captain of the battleship, although supposed to be French, has no accent and is not especially French in appearance.

A French girl, reporter for a European newspaper, is shown as pretty, nicely dressed, with a very vivacious manner and a decided accent.

Four English men and 2 English women, a total of 6, were classified as humorous. Fifty per cent of the remaining 8 characters were classified as attractive. Their descriptions follow:

Hodgkins, a steamship steward, is short and stocky in appear
ance. very affable and philosophical, and speaks with a broad
Cockney accent.

Larry, the hero, is an English song composer, but differs little
from an American in either appearance or accent.

The Bishop, an English clergyman, is a kindly man of about
sixty, with no outstanding racial characteristics.

Eustace, an English lord, is a humorous character, monocled,
silly and simpering. His speech is not so heavily accented but
his phrases and speech mannerisms are supposedly typically
English.

Gemma, an English girl who is carrying on an intrigue with
the heroine's husband, seems American in speech and appearance.

Tarneverro, a mystic and crystal gazer, is English, although
he attempts to give an impression of East Indian or Oriental
origin.

Aunt Prunella, an English aristocrat, is shown as snobbish
and fortune-hunting, but in appearance and speech she displays
no traits which could be considered typically English.

The Duchess is a large woman, very much overdressed, who
speaks in a bored and brusque voice.

Anna, the English maid, has no outstanding racial characteristics.

Mr. Adkins, an English tailor, while evidently extremely
wealthy, is mean and grasping, but is not strikingly English in
either appearance or accent.

Elinor, who belongs to an aristocratic English family, seems
no different from an American girl in appearance or speech.

Fin, a steward on a freighter, is a Cockney Englishman, small,
alert, invariably dropping his h's.

Ronnie Kilkerry, an English lord, is portrayed as an attractive
rotter, but is given none of the supposedly typical English
attributes.

Sue, an English girl and a friend of the heroine, evidences no
outstandingly English characteristics.

Four Jews were classified as humorous, 3 men and 1 woman. One Jew was classified as attractive; none as unattractive.

The Negroes and the Swedes share honors for third place as humorous characters, 5 Swedes being shown in this light, all men, and 5 Negroes, 3 men and 2 women. One Swede was shown as non-humorous and unattractive, while 1 Negro was shown as non-humorous and attractive. Descriptions of the Swedish characters follow:

> Ole Olsen, a steamship officer, is shown as slow of comprehension, gullible, and somewhat shy. He is very Scandinavian in appearance, but beyond speaking very slowly, does not have much accent.
>
> Axel Bronstrup, one of the students at a preparatory school, looks very Swedish, is slow and plodding in school, socially backward, and hesitant in speech.
>
> Ole, a cowboy and friend of the hero, is almost a burlesque type of Swede, with a very heavy accent, and furnishes much of the comedy relief.
>
> Axel, the janitor, is very Swedish in appearance, speaks hesitantly with a heavy accent, and yet is rather shrewd in business matters.
>
> Ole, one of the theater audience, is Swedish in appearance and accent, laughably slow of comprehension, and displays very bad manners.
>
> Sigrid Carlene, a Swedish dancer, has no trace of accent but betrays her race in her appearance.

These last data indicate unmistakably the use of foreign characters to furnish comedy relief, since out of a total of 102 characters of foreign or colored extraction, 50 of them, or approximately 50 per cent, were definitely humorous characters.

Table 18 indicates the occupations of the various members of other races and nationalities. It is evident at once that we are not going to see depicted the best of other races and nationalities in terms of occupations. Indeed, 14 of the 102 characters have no occupation, and 13 have an unknown occupation. Twelve belong to the nobility or royalty. We see, therefore, that the understanding which these 40 pictures give of the workaday world of the foreign or non-white races is indeed meager, when we discover that 51 of them, or exactly one half, are included under "no occupation," "unknown occupation," "nobility and royalty," or "soldier."

Especially significant is the fact that of the 6 American Negroes shown, 4 were servants and 2 theatrical attendants. We shall have to look long before we discover in the movies a portrayal of men of the type of Booker T. Washington, Countee Cullen, Paul Robeson, and Roland Hayes. The Negro in the movies is, almost without exception, either an entertainer or a servant of white folks.

It is evident that a sampling of 40 pictures is inadequate to catch that relatively small number of pictures produced each year which deal almost exclusively with certain foreign groups. The cycle of Chinese films is an example. In 1932 and 1933 we had "Charlie Chan's Chance," "Son-Daughter," "Shanghai Express," "The Bitter Tea of General Yen," and "The Mask of Fu Manchu."

It is possible, however, that we have disposed of the question of unattractiveness too simply. It is highly possible that motion pictures might produce a more favorable attitude toward a race, as depicted by the Thurstone scale, yet be objected to very strenuously by the race portrayed in that picture. For example, the depicting of a Negro as a kindly, thoughtful servant may shift attitudes toward the more favorable side of the scale, yet be objected to by Negroes who feel that the constant showing of the Negro as a menial servant is prejudicial to their race.

TABLE 18

OCCUPATIONS IN WHICH PERSONS OF THE DIFFERENT NATIONALITIES WERE SHOWN IN THE 40 PICTURES

Number of persons of each nationality engaged in each occupation

Occupation	French	English	Russian	Am. Negro	Swedish	Jewish	German	Moroccan	N. Am. Indian	Austrian	Italian	Irish	Spanish	Mexican	Sumatran	Japanese	Chinese	Scotch	Hungarian	Portuguese	Turkish	Cuban	Hawaiian	Total
No occupation	1	2	2				2	1	1			1	1		1			1					1	14
Occup. unknown	5						3	3		2														13
Nobility—Royalty	3	5	3						1															12
Soldier	2		4			5			1															12
Servant		1		4																				5
Proprietor	1										1									1	1	1		5
Govt.—Civic official	2							1																3
Theatrical attendant				2															1					3
Detective												1				1	1							3
Naval officer	2																							2
Steward			2																					2
Theater manager					2																			2
Prostitute—Mistress			1											1										2
Bandit		2																						2
Scout—Hunter											1				1									2
Farmer—Planter													1			1								2
Military aide					1																			1
Spy											1													1
Steamship officer					1																			1
Waitress														1										1
Janitor					1																			1
Trainer												1												1
Barber	1																							1
Tailor		1																						1
Lawyer					1																			1
Clergyman		1																						1
Artist	1																							1
Composer		1																						1
Entertainer	1																							1
Dancer										1														1
Crystal gazer		1																						1
Cowboy									1															1
Student										1														1
Reporter	1																							1
Total	20	14	12	6	6	5	5	5	4	4	3	3	2	2	2	2	1	1	1	1	1	1	1	102

Further, although some of the Chinese characters in the films mentioned above were depicted in a favorable light as judged by an Occidental observer, a thoughtful Chinese student, a Ph.D. of one of our state universities, objected strongly to the picture these films gave of his race.

We see, therefore, that while a specific depiction of a person may be accurate, yet by its very emphasis on this type of character and its failure to emphasize the better members of that race it may set up harmful prejudice. For example, according to an item in the *World Telegram* for May 13, 1931, a dinner was arranged by Generose Pope, Italian publisher, for the purpose of discouraging the movie industry from portraying gunmen and racketeers as Italians. Perhaps protest from such groups as these is the best answer to an industry which makes its living from profits. If profits can be menaced by pressure groups, then inaccurate and unattractive portrayals may cease.

But the parent who has the problem of deciding whether to send his child to the movies may still be puzzled. What can he do? Certainly he will avoid sending his children to those which are patently prejudicial. He may well protest to producers for depicting races by their worst representatives. And further, he can make use of those motion pictures which do give an honest understanding of foreign persons and underprivileged groups.

SUMMARY

The study of the movie characters was also based on the 115 pictures which were actually viewed and the 40 of these which were studied in greater detail.

The leading characters are, for the most part, in their twenties. The female characters are younger than the male characters, and of the latter the villains are older than the heroes. The longest age range is found in the group designated as *other men*, although this group exceeds that of *other women* by but one interval. None of the heroines was over

35, while the oldest hero was less than 56. One villain was in his 60's while a villainess was between 56 and 60.

A little less than one half of all the characters were seen to be in what is called "moderate circumstances." Thirty-seven per cent of the characters were seen in the two wealthier categories, and 12 per cent were considered poor. In the wealthy and ultra-wealthy categories are found a larger percentage of villains and villainesses than heroes and heroines.

The leading characters are seen in 22 occupations, though more characters are shown having no occupation than are shown engaging in any one type of occupation. This number may be high, however, as approximately 50 per cent of the women tabulated as having no occupation were married. If being married had been considered as an occupation for women the total number of unoccupied characters would be reduced to about 70, which would change the rank of *no occupation* from first to fifth. *Commercial* ranked second, *illegal*, third; *occupation unknown*, fourth; and *theatrical*, fifth.

Forty-nine per cent of the characters from the 23 foreign nationalities depicted were shown as humorous, 34 per cent as non-humorous and attractive, and 17 per cent as non-humorous and unattractive.

Study of the characters leads us to infer that certain problems of young adulthood are the ones treated by the movies. Is this socially desirable? It is possible that the most vital and dramatic problems of life arise before 30. It is equally possible that the movies are doing definite harm in indicating that by the time one attains the age of 30 all one's problems will have been solved. As it may be desirable for the adolescent to view the problems he will encounter in the next decade, it may also be desirable for the 20-year-old to glimpse the problems of the 30's and 40's. One entirely delightful motion picture dealt with the problem of what a man should do with his time after he had retired from business. It seems to the writer that there may be many such problems which would lend themselves to motion-picture presentation.

That the movies are but slightly concerned with the work of the world is brought out in the study of characters, as it was in settings. Many of the leading characters appeared to have no occupation, or their occupation was so unimportant to the plot it was impossible to tell what it was. However, a variety of occupations was presented. The emphasis on crime is again shown, in that illegal occupations ranked high.

In the portrayal of characters the movies fall down rather badly when it comes to foreigners. Probably one of the reasons that humorous characters are so often portrayed as foreign is that that which is strange is apt to be humorous. It may take less cleverness to be funny with a dialect. To accept the movie foreign character as typical, however, would indicate that in comparison with the rest of the world America was quite deficient in humorous persons.

CHAPTER V

AN ANALYSIS OF THE CLOTHING WORN BY LEADING CHARACTERS

"Dresses for breakfasts, and dinners, and balls,
Dresses to sit in, and stand in, and walk in,
Dresses to dance in, and flirt in, and talk in,
Dresses in which to do nothing at all;
Dresses for winter, spring, summer, and fall,
All of them different in color and shape,
Silk, muslin, and lace, velvet, satin, and crepe,
Brocade and broadcloth, and other material,
Quite as expensive, and much more ethereal. . . ."
WM. ALLEN BUTLER—"Nothing to Wear"

The material in this chapter deals with clothing and shows the important connection between what is shown on the screen and its influence on the type and nature of clothing worn by the public. This is clearly demonstrated in other of the Payne Fund studies. Doctors Shuttleworth and May, for example, found that:

The movie children tend to say that "A little rouge, high heels, and smart clothes add to the attractiveness of a girl," that "Good clothes help to make the man," and that "All" or "Most" "smartly dressed girls are popular," "attractive girls wear smart clothes," "children would stay away from a party rather than wear shabby clothes." [1]

The following statements, collected by Dr. Blumer, also indicate the great influence which the motion picture exerts in this area.

Male, white, 20, robbery, inmate of reformatory.—When I see a movie that shows snappy clothes, big cars, and lots of money, it

[1] Shuttleworth, Frank K., and May, Mark A., *The Social Conduct and Attitudes of Movie Fans*, New York: The Macmillan Company, 1933, p. 58.

66

makes me want to have them too. It makes me ashamed of my own clothes and wish I had clothes like theirs.[2]

Female, 19, white, college junior.—I am always more interested in what the heroine wears than in what she does. Most dresses worn in movies are too striking or too elaborate for me to copy, but where there is shown a different collar, a pretty cuff, or a novel trimming it is certain to crop out in some dress.[3]

Female, 16, white, high-school junior.—Most likely if it weren't for the movies we would wait a long time for styles to change. I copy all the collegiate styles from the movies. In "Wild Party," starring Clara Bow, she wears a kind of sleeveless jumper dress which attracted my attention very much. Nothing could be done about it. My mother had to buy me one just like it.[3]

Female, 16, white, high-school junior.—No, I don't think that I have ever imitated any stars in their manners. But I remember after having seen "Our Dancing Daughters" with Joan Crawford, I wanted a dress exactly like one she had worn in a certain scene. It was a very "flapper" type of dress, and I don't usually go in for that sort of thing.[3]

Male, 20, white, college sophomore.—The appearance of such handsome men as John Gilbert, Ben Lyon, Gilbert Roland, and the host of others, dressed in sport clothes, evening attire, formals, etc., has encouraged me to dress as best possible in order to make similar appearance.[3]

Indeed, the devious methods used to make Americans clothes-conscious, and especially "movie-clothes"-conscious, are worthy of thorough and detailed study by those who are interested in the concept of imitation. Our purpose in this chapter will be only to introduce the problem and to present some of the data which have been discovered.

The motion-picture producers have been intensely aware of the screen as an advertising medium. Clothing copied from

[2] Blumer, Herbert, and Hauser, Philip M., *Movies, Delinquency, and Crime*, New York: The Macmillan Company, 1933, p. 45.
[3] Blumer, Herbert, *Movies and Conduct*, New York: The Macmillan Company, 1933, pp. 31–34.

that worn by the stars is sold in department stores, usually
as a tie-up to fit in with the time the picture is released. For
example, on January 22, 1933, the *Columbus Dispatch* carried
the following news item:

FASHIONS OF FILM STARS AVAILABLE

Morehouse Martens Offers Same Styles
Worn by Players in Movies

The thrill of walking into a theater showing Joan Crawford's
latest screen triumph, while wearing a dress identical with the
one the actress wears, is a Columbus department store's latest
appeal for women and girls. Morehouse Martens has just completed an arrangement by which copies of movie stars' clothes
are on sale at the store prior to or coincident with the opening of
their pictures.

Four Leading Stylists

Four outstanding dress designers in Hollywood are recognized
by stylists. Best known is Adrian, who dresses Garbo, Crawford,
and Shearer among others.

Orrey-Kelley of First National is winning a reputation, as is
Travis Banton of Paramount and De Lima of RKO.

These leading fashion creators of Hollywood are all men.
Chanel, of Paris, spent a period in Hollywood last year. Her
influence is declared to have been effective in simplifying and
improving the taste of movie clothes.

Copies Now Ready

At Morehouse Martens there are now ready copies of a Joan
Blondell double-duty dress, a Jean Arthur frock and Claire
Dodd pajamas.

February "Photoplay" displays these same creations in the
.fashion section.

As demonstrated here, a unique advertising tie-up is
arranged through screen magazines. Let's glance at the

February, 1933 issue of *Photoplay*. First we find, on page 93, a full-page advertisement enlivened with cuts of movie frocks. At the top is pictured a pretty girl, holding aloft a cocktail glass, and the reading matter runs as follows:

NOW! WEAR HOLLYWOOD'S CLEVER CLOTHES!

Out of motion pictures come the smartest of fashions; dainty frocks, charming coats, gayest of sportswear created for your favorite stars in latest picture plays. Now, you, too, may wear these clever clothes—for exact copies are offered at moderate prices by many confidence-commanding stores! If you do not know where to buy "Hollywood Fashions" ask PHOTOPLAY, using the coupon printed for your convenience below.

Each month Seymour, stylist for PHOTOPLAY MAGAZINE, presents the newest "Hollywood Fashions." Read about them in PHOTOPLAY; see them on the screen in local theaters; add them to your own wardrobe!

In another section of the same issue, six pages of illustrations of "Hollywood Fashions" are presented. Here are a few excerpts from the descriptions which accompany them:

Carole Lombard knows how to choose smart clothes and wear them well both on and off the screen. In "No Man of Her Own," she plays the rôle of a young librarian who marries a man of means—as you can imagine, this gives her a grand opportunity to wear some stunning costumes. One of them is this attractive black crepe dress trimmed in white.

When you see "Hot Pepper," look for this attractive evening gown worn by Lilian Bond. Earl Luick designed it for a night-club scene.

Lovely Jean Arthur has returned to the screen in "The Past of Mary Holmes." Walter Plunkett has used a shell pink ratine for this graceful gown which she wears at a dinner party in her home.

The following advertisement concludes the display:

HOLLYWOOD FASHIONS

sponsored by PHOTOPLAY MAGAZINE and worn by famous stars in latest motion pictures now may be secured for your own wardrobe from leading department and ready-to-wear stores in many localities. . . .

Faithful copies of these smartly styled and moderately-priced garments, of which those shown in this issue of PHOTOPLAY are typical, are on display this month in the stores of those representative merchants whose firm names are conveniently listed on Page 123.

Moreover, some of the widely circulated women's magazines are now presenting patterns of frocks worn by motion-picture stars, carefully timing these advertisements so that they reach the public just previous to the release date of the picture in which these clothes are worn.

Another type of tie-up with the department stores is indicated by the following quotation from the "press book" [4] on Gloria Swanson's picture "Indiscreet":

Unsurpassed in the wearing of beautiful and appropriate clothes, Gloria Swanson makes a distinct appeal to women patrons in this particular. True to her custom, the popular star exhibits in "Indiscreet" a variety of costumes that will be discussed by your female patrons for weeks after the picture closes at your theater. You should cash in on this situation by telling the facts to the manager of a department or women's wear store, and arranging for a Fashion Show, and the exploitation of Gloria's flair for dress, and the current offerings of the store. Here are two suggestions:

Stills Nos. 118, 143, 149, 135, 159 show the number and variety of costumes worn by the star in "Indiscreet." Secure a set of these from your Exchange and have enlargements made and mounted or framed as you see fit. Have the store put on a double or triple window Gloria Swanson Dress Display or Fashion Display, of the same styles of garments as are shown in the stills.

[4] A "press book" is the book of publicity and sample advertisements which the producer sends out to the exhibitor with each picture.

Display a still showing a ball gown with the store's selection, the sport costume still with the store's model, and so on throughout the series.   Arrange for a tie-up that will feature these garments this way: "10 per cent discount on all these Gloria Swanson models from (date) to (date) while the best dressed star in pictures is appearing at the Blank Theater in 'Indiscreet.' Now is your opportunity to show discretion."

Another: Arrange with the Fashion or Home Department of a newspaper to conduct a Fashion Designing Contest.   Fashion Drawings to be submitted for prizes.   The paper should carry reproductions of the winning drawings and portraits of the winners.

In the same press book we have also the following statement:

PAJAMA FAD STARTED BY GLORIA SWANSON

If there still remains any doubt as to the growing vogue of pajamas as a daytime costume for women, proponents of the idea will find evidence to support their argument in Gloria Swanson's enthusiastic adoption of the attire during the production of her latest United Artists picture, "Indiscreet," which comes to the . . . Theater next week.

In addition to choosing smart pajamas of black and cream satin as her costume in one of the major sequences of the picture, the star wore the trousered lounging ensembles almost constantly during the filming of the entire production.

For the short drive to the studio from her home in Beverly Hills, she usually wore pajama costumes of chiffon velvet in various shades, with blouses of neutral tones.   And for wear in her studio bungalow, at story conferences, rehearsals and in the projection room, pajamas were the preferred habiliment.

The motion picture becomes, therefore, in the eyes of producers something of a fashion show.   They believe that women will be induced to attend the theaters in the hope that they will see displayed there clothing which is smart and new for the season.   Whether this overemphasis on the matter of clothing is likely to set up false standards of living, and induce luxury standards where more modest standards should prevail, is not the province of this investigation. It is evident, however, that the motion pictures with their tie-ups with department stores have a definite effect upon the clothing standards of the nation. Parents and educators, especially those instructors in home economics who are concerned with teaching youth to purchase clothing that is

TABLE 19

TYPE OF CLOTHING WORN BY CHARACTERS IN THE 40 PICTURES

Number and per cent of pictures in which characters were shown in each type of clothing

Type of Clothing	Men		Women		Either or Both Men or Women	
	Number	Per cent	Number	Per cent	Number	Per cent
Informal clothing..........	37	93	37	93	39	98
Occupational clothing......	39	98	27	68	39	98
Intimate clothing..........	21	53	24	60	30	75
Formal clothing	27	68	27	68	29	73
Recreational clothing.......	14	35	20	50	22	55
Costumes.................	11	28	12	30	14	35
Children's clothing.........	10	25	2	5	11	28
Humorous clothing	6	15	2	5	7	18
Furs.....................	3	8	4	10	5	13
Academic clothing.........	2	5	2	5	2	5

appropriate for the occasion and adjusted to the economic status of the individual, may well pause and consider the degree to which their training is facilitated or thwarted through the motion picture's emphasis on clothing.

Forty pictures were analyzed in detail to discover the nature of the clothing worn not only by the leading characters but also by other characters who had minor parts. Minor characters were included because we were interested in obtaining data on occupational clothing of various types which in many cases was not worn by what we have considered leading characters. Types of clothing were not tabulated by individual characters because these characters were constantly appearing in different types of dress and a great deal of duplication resulted.

The general conclusions are presented in Table 19. The table is read as follows: In 37 of the 40 pictures, or 93 per cent, there were men who wore informal clothing. In 37 pictures, or 93 per cent, women were seen wearing informal clothing. In 39 pictures, or 98 per cent, either or both men or women were shown wearing informal clothing. It will be noted that this is slightly higher than the per cent for the men or the women, since it is evident that there will be some pictures in which one of the sexes will be seen in informal clothing, while the other sex will not be represented.

Each of these subheads is further reclassified, and these data are here presented and discussed.

Intimate Clothing

The following facts can be discovered in Table 20. If the 40 pictures analyzed in detail adequately represent all motion pictures made in that year, anyone who attended a motion picture would have about one chance in four of seeing a leading woman character in her underwear, and one chance in 40 of seeing a man in his underwear. Just why the motion-picture producers hold such a strong prejudice against the male figure attired in underwear is not made clear by these data.

That characters do a good deal of lounging around in the movies is illustrated by the fact that in 40 per cent of the pictures either leading male or female characters are shown in negligee or in dressing gowns.

Night clothing is a popular attire for movie actors and actresses, being discovered in 40 per cent of the pictures which we analyzed in detail. Almost equal proportions of men and women are shown in night clothing.

Bathing, that is taking a bath (if this can be referred to as a clothing situation) appeared in only two of the 40 pictures,

TABLE 20

Intimate Clothing Situations and Intimate Clothing Worn by Characters in the 40 Pictures

Number and per cent of pictures in which characters were shown in each type of clothing or clothing situation

Type of Clothing or Situation	Men		Women		Either or Both Men or Women	
	Number	Per cent	Number	Per cent	Number	Per cent
Clothing						
Underwear.............	1	3	10	25	11	28
Negligee and dressing gown................	8	20	12	30	16	40
Night clothing..........	11	28	10	25	16	40
Revealing clothing.......	8	20	18	45	23	58
Situation						
Bathing (taking a bath)..	0	0	2	5	2	5
Dressing................	4	10	5	13	9	23
Undressing.............	5	13	9	23	12	30
Total....................	21	53	24	60	30	75

or 5 per cent. In both cases, the bathing situation involved women characters.

Dressing scenes were found in 23 per cent and undressing scenes were found in 30 per cent of the 40 pictures. Almost twice as many pictures showed scenes of women undressing as showed scenes of men undressing. Further, women were shown undressing in about one fourth of the pictures.

Revealing clothing was shown in 58 per cent of the pic-

tures.   Forty-five per cent of the pictures included women
in revealing clothing, and 20 per cent of the pictures included
men.   Revealing clothing includes certain of the dressing and
undressing situations noted in the table and any clothing
(usually women's) which is cut extremely low in front or
back, which is unusually short, or which is more or less
transparent, revealing legs and outline of the figure.   In
addition to being classified as "revealing" the clothing in
question is also listed under any other category into which
it would ordinarily fall.   That is, if a nightgown worn by a
character is decided to be "revealing," it is classified there
and also under "night clothing."

Since the term "revealing clothing" is somewhat indefinite, some of the actual situations noted in these cases are
here reported.

Professor Willow explains that Axel is accustomed to take a
daily sun bath on the roof of the laundry "in what I may roughly
call 'the nude.'"   At this moment, Axel, clad only in a bath
towel draped about his waist, appears cautiously above the
parapet of the laundry roof.

As soon as the door closes, the Countess removes her coat,
revealing the fact that she is clad only in a chemise and shoes
and stockings.   The conductor knocks at the door of the train
compartment and while the Countess is talking with him, she
draws herself up haughtily, loosening her fur coat, which falls
open and reveals her embroidered silk chemise. She notices the
conductor staring at her, realizes that she is not dressed, and
pulls her coat together, laughing nervously.

Sigrid, wearing a white negligee trimmed in black fur, crosses
and stands in front of the long mirror, the light outlining her
legs through her negligee.

Mrs. Flint has crossed to her dressing-table, slipped off her
dress, displaying a white foundation garment, consisting of a

combined girdle, brassiere, and step-ins, and is putting on a dark lounging robe.

Connie, bare legs visible below a swinging door, and bare shoulders showing above, is taking a shower in a little shower room off the dining room of the cabin. Presently she emerges with a towel wrapped about her, warning, "No fair peeking."

Occupational Clothing

Data on the occupational clothing worn in the movies may give clues, perhaps slight, as to the various occupations which persons enter. Further, they may suggest rather strongly the absence or presence in motion pictures of groups which emphasize social superiorities and inferiorities. Table 21 presents this information.

The first category under this heading is *uniforms*, which has been subdivided still further. *Military* uniforms, besides including ordinary Army uniforms, takes in cadet uniforms worn at West Point, also uniforms of armies of other countries, such as the French Foreign Legion. The categories *naval* and *merchant marine* uniforms are self-explanatory.

Aviation uniforms are clothing worn by aviators not only in the government air service, but also commercial pilots and private individuals.

Under the heading *police* uniforms, is included not only police officers, but sheriffs, marshals, and the like. Detectives, or plain clothes men, are not dealt with here, however, as their clothing does not indicate their profession.

Attendants' uniforms is a broad category and is used in apposition to *domestic servants'* uniforms. An attendant is construed as anyone giving service in a public place, *i.e.*, waiters, ushers, conductors, doormen, taxi-drivers, and the like. The other category, *domestic servants'* uniforms, needs no explanation.

Professional dress includes such clothing as the white coats or uniforms worn by nurses, doctors, dentists, and so forth, in the performance of their professional duties.

TABLE 21

OCCUPATIONAL CLOTHING WORN BY CHARACTERS IN THE 40 PICTURES

Number and per cent of pictures in which characters were shown in each type of occupational clothing

Type of Clothing	Men		Women		Either or Both Men or Women	
	Num-ber	Per cent	Num-ber	Per cent	Num-ber	Per cent
Uniforms						
Military...............	9	23	1	3	9	23
Naval.................	4	10	0	0	4	10
Merchant marine........	6	15	0	0	6	15
Aviation...............	4	10	2	5	5	13
Police.................	11	28	0	0	11	28
Prison.................	2	5	1	3	3	8
Attendants'............	24	60	6	15	26	65
Domestic servants'	20	50	12	30	22	55
Professional dress.........	3	8	2	5	5	13
Professional sports clothing.	1	3	0	0	1	3
Ecclesiastical dress........	5	13	2	5	6	15
Theatrical costumes........	3	8	7	18	7	18
Western clothing..........	4	10	1	3	4	10
Work clothing						
Overalls—Jumpers.......	5	13	0	0	5	13
Rough, heavy clothing...	5	13	1	3	5	13
Total..................	39	98	27	68	39 [a]	98 [a]

[a] "Rango," using only natives as leading characters, is not represented here.

Professional sports clothing includes clothing worn by persons when engaged in professional sports such as prize-fighting, horse racing, and so on.

Eccesiastical dress takes in not only clerical dress and robes, but Salvation Army uniforms, evangelistic robes, and the like. *Theatrical costumes* are self-explanatory. *Western clothing* consists of the usual "chaps," sombrero, checkered shirt, spurred boots, and the like, worn by the typical cowboy. *Work clothing*, with its subheads of *overalls and jumpers* and *rough, heavy clothing* needs no further qualification.

The fact that in 55 per cent of the pictures we see domestic servants in their appropriate uniforms reveals the motion picture as placing heavy emphasis upon standards of living far beyond the level of the group of persons who see such pictures.

It should be pointed out here that the data on domestic servants were gathered not in relation to only the leading characters but include all domestic servants found in the 40 pictures. As a matter of fact, only 5 out of 133 heroes were servants, and 4 out of 130 heroines were servants. The pattern set up as attractive, therefore, is that of the master or mistress, not that of the servant.

When the writer determined the number of pictures in which *either* a military or a naval uniform was noted, he discovered that 13 out of the 40 pictures had characters presented in either one or the other of these uniforms. This fact, that approximately one third of the pictures presented characters in military or naval uniform, reënforces the data brought out later in an analysis of newsreels, that there is an emphasis on war situations.

Formal Clothing

Table 22 presents the data on the formal attire worn in the 40 pictures. The categories under this heading are more or less self-explanatory. *Morning dress*, used in reference to men's clothing, usually consists of a frock coat and light or striped trousers, and sometimes a high silk hat. *Formal pajamas*, used in reference to women's clothing, are pajamas which are worn in place of an evening gown. *Wedding gowns* are considered formal if they do not fall into a distinctly informal classification, as, for example, a simple silk dress worn for a very small and informal wedding.

TABLE 22

FORMAL CLOTHING WORN BY CHARACTERS IN THE 40 PICTURES

Number and per cent of pictures in which characters were shown in each type of formal clothing

Type of Clothing	Either or Both Men or Women	
	Number	Per cent
Men		
Full dress	13	33
Dinner jacket	18	45
High hat	17	43
Morning dress	13	33
Women		
Evening gown	27	68
Formal pajamas	1	3
Evening wrap	20	50
Wedding gown	3	8
Total	29	73

The data in this table on formal clothing needs little comment. The fact that in 68 per cent of the pictures women were shown in evening gowns and that in 50 per cent of the pictures leading women characters are shown in an evening wrap, further emphasizes the luxury standards of motion pictures. The emphasis on formal clothing of men reënforces that which was just presented for women.

It is not the function of the investigator to speculate at length on the social implications of these data. Combined with the data on wealthy and ultra-wealthy settings they serve strikingly to show that motion-picture producers believe that what the public wants to see is something beyond their lives. They demonstrate that the producers believe that audiences can be attracted by emphasizing the recreational activities of the rich. Many argue that the producers are correct in that assumption. The social desirability of this appeal is another question.

Informal Clothing

The data on informal clothing are presented in Table 23 without comment.

TABLE 23

INFORMAL CLOTHING WORN BY CHARACTERS IN THE 40 PICTURES

Number and per cent of pictures in which characters were shown in each type of informal clothing

Type of Clothing	Men		Women		Either or Both Men or Women	
	Number	Per cent	Number	Per cent	Number	Per cent
Business or street clothing..	31	78	34	85	37	93
General informal clothing ..	27	68	22	55	30	75
Semi-formal clothing.......	4	10	18	45	19	48
Domestic dress...........	1	3	9	23	10	25
Lounging dress...........	1	3	6	15	7	18
Heavy, outdoor clothing ...	1	3	1	3	1	3
Total...................	37	93	37	93	39	98

The description of each type of clothing follows:

Business or street clothing includes both men's and women's clothing which is suitable for wear in an office, on the street, or for traveling. Under the heading *semi-formal clothing* is classified afternoon or evening dress which is not distinctly formal but which is too elaborate for street or business wear.

General informal clothing is perhaps the broadest category. All clothing which does not fall distinctly into any other class is put here. For example, if a man is wearing an ordinary business suit, but is in his shirtsleeves, his clothing will be classified under the above category. *General informal clothing* is used as opposed to *business or street clothing* and *sport clothing*. But its distinction from these two is usually clear-cut, and it does not approach any categories other than these.

Lounging dress consists almost wholly of lounging pajamas, but also includes men's smoking jackets. *Domestic dress* refers to house-dresses, aprons, and smocks.

Heavy outdoor clothing is that worn for winter sports and in the northern part of the country, usually consisting of such articles as mackinaws, toboggan caps, trousers tucked into boots, and the like.

Recreational Clothing

Table 24 presents the essential data on recreational clothing.

TABLE 24

Recreational Clothing Worn by Characters in the 40 Pictures

Number and per cent of pictures in which characters were shown in each type of recreational clothing

Type of Clothing	Men		Women		Either or Both Men or Women	
	Number	Per cent	Number	Per cent	Number	Per cent
Sport clothing............	11	28	14	35	17	43
Bathing suits	4	10	5	13	5	13
Beach wear...............	3	8	5	13	5	13
Riding habits	1	3	5	13	5	13
Athletic uniforms..........	2	5	0	0	2	5
Total...................	14	35	20	50	22	55

Beach wear includes beach robes, beach pajamas, and the like, while the category *bathing suits* is self-explanatory.

Sport clothing as a separate category takes in a fairly definite type of dress. Here are placed men's knicker suits, which, although technically worn for golf and similar sports, are widely used as simply an informal type of clothing. In addition, other men's clothing included here are "white flannels," "white ducks," sweaters, and the like. This same classification holds in regard to women's dress, including clothing suitable for golf and tennis, sweaters and skirts, and similar attire.

Riding habits needs no explanation, but a jockey's uniform would be placed under *professional sports clothing* rather than here.

Athletic uniforms include all clothing of this type, particularly football, baseball, basketball, track, and similar uniforms. But any uniform worn for what is known as a *professional sport*, such as prize-fighting, wrestling, and so on, is listed under the heading of *professional sports clothing*.

Other Types of Clothing

An analysis was also made of other types of clothing, including academic robes, school uniforms, masquerade costumes, historical costumes, fur coats, and native costumes. Of these, native costumes are the only ones which appear often enough to justify inclusion. They appear in 25 per cent of the pictures. This is easily accounted for by the fact that 40 per cent of the 115 pictures had a locale that was either wholly or partly foreign.

A phenomenon worthy of comment is the fact that nearly every leading character looks as though he or she just came out of a bandbox. The clothing is clean, well pressed, fresh-looking—too fresh-looking, perhaps. William S. Cunningham of the *Columbus Citizen* puts it this way:

> . . . Hollywood strives so much for perfection that their attempts boomerang and become artificial.
>
> Particularly, in this respect, does Hollywood strive for physical

perfection. Almost every woman in the American films—from "extra" to star—is pretty if not beautiful. Most every man, if not handsome, is well-groomed.

Complexions are flawless. There are no men needing shaves. Clothes fit well. Thanks to expert make-up men, expert lighting, expert costuming, the result is perfect. I'm afraid it's too perfect.

Of course, this doesn't apply universally. There are some homely women in pictures, there are some shipwrecked heroes who look like bums. But most of them bear the instantly recognized stamp of "character actor" or just "actor." In many cases, they're too perfect bums.

I'm not campaigning for sloppy imperfection or asking that the movies strip their stories of glamour. And I most certainly am not waging any war against pretty women.

But I do feel that the Hollywood product could be improved by striving for real realism.[5]

Summary

The study of clothing was based on the 40 pictures which were studied in detail. Clothing worn by leading and minor characters was considered.

It is difficult to draw conclusions from the data in the study of clothing. To say that a leading character appeared in an evening gown does not indicate whether that gown cost $20 or $200. All these pictures were actually viewed and it may be said that the clothing decidedly added to the impression that the leading characters belonged to the wealthier class.

Both from the evidence presented here and from that in other studies of this series it is seen that the clothing in the movies influences the styles. Those who are interested in cultivating the art of tasteful and suitable dress cannot neglect the influence of the movies.

[5] April 4, 1933.

Informal and *occupational clothing* was seen in practically all of the pictures. *Intimate clothing* was seen in three fourths, *formal clothing* in a little less than three fourths, and *recreational clothing* in over one half of the pictures. Other types of clothing seen were *costumes, children's clothing, humorous clothing, furs,* and *academic clothing.*

Although women in intimate clothing were seen in but a few more pictures than were men similarly attired, they were seen in many more situations. Fifteen types of occupational clothing were shown, of which over one half were uniforms. Informal clothing was divided among six types, of which business or street clothing was seen most often. Recreational clothing of five types was seen. These types in order of rank by the number of pictures in which they were seen were: *sport clothing, bathing suits, beach wear, riding habits,* and *athletic uniforms.*

CHAPTER VI

CIRCUMSTANCES OF MEETING AND LOVEMAKING

CIRCUMSTANCES OF MEETING

WHAT pattern does the motion picture set up for youth in reference to ways in which they will meet persons whom they may later marry? Are these methods of acquaintance-ship shown as primarily accidental and unusual, or do they show that one's choice of a mate is usually conditioned by the persons with whom he ordinarily associates? Does the motion picture frown upon pick-ups on the beach, the street, or at dances, or does it show them as desirable? Does it ever show harmful consequences of irregular methods of acquaintanceship, or are love affairs and marriage resulting from such an acquaintanceship often shown as highly successful?

In this analysis of the circumstances under which characters meet we have limited our study to the hero and the heroine. It is evident, of course, that there are love relationships between leading characters other than the hero and heroine, but we have not included these. Moreover, we have further limited our data to include only those heroes and heroines between whom there has been some sort of love relationship.

These characters have been divided into two groups—*previously acquainted* and *not previously acquainted*. The term *previously acquainted* means those who have been acquainted before the opening of the picture. This is divided

into three categories of: *acquainted, engaged,* and *married.*
Under *not previously acquainted* the methods that are used to
secure such an acquaintanceship are *with introduction* or
without introduction in a *usual situation* or in an *unusual situation.* A situation is considered *unusual* when there is little
chance of a young person encountering it in real life.

One picture contained no heroine, and therefore was not
tabulated. In 13 of the remaining 39 pictures the hero
and heroine are previously acquainted. In 3 of the 13 pictures they are shown as engaged, and in 2 as married. In
the 26 pictures in which they are not acquainted at the
beginning of the picture, in 11 they are introduced, in 15
they are not introduced, in 9 meet in a usual situation, and
in 17 in an unusual situation. Emphasis is therefore placed
on the unusual meeting. A description of these 17 unusual
meetings follows:

> The heroine mistakes the hero for a young man with whom
> she and her aunt have a dinner engagement, and begins to dance
> on the sidewalk with him.
>
> The hero, who is the leader of an outlaw band, first sees the
> heroine when she is kidnapped by one of his men and brought to
> the outlaw camp.
>
> Upon finding that the heroine has lassoed his horse, the hero,
> mistaking her for another cowboy, kicks her in the seat of the
> trousers.
>
> The hero, an escaped prisoner of war, meets the heroine while
> she is living in a hut in the midst of the forest with a group of
> other fugitives, all men except herself.
>
> The hero, who is the proprietor of a radio shop, takes some
> radio batteries up to a large, isolated house one stormy night.
> The atmosphere of the whole place is distinctly scary, and he
> loses his bearings and goes down a hall without the butler, who
> was guiding him. Suddenly a door opens and a pretty girl
> appears and begs him to help her, as she is in terrible trouble,

then she immediately declares that she has to get out of there and disappears through another door.

The hero first sees the heroine in a café where she is an entertainer. By a ruse he lures her escort away, then pretends that the other man has asked him to look after her while he is gone.

The hero, a fugitive from justice, enters the heroine's inn-room *via* the window.

The hero is in danger of being jailed, so his two friends persuade the heroine to pose as his newly married wife in order to work upon the sympathies of the marshal and obtain the hero's release.

The hero, a county sheriff, kills the heroine's brother, who is a bandit. When the heroine arrives in town, planning to live with her brother, she is brought to the hero's office and he is forced to tell her that her brother is dead.

The hero saves the heroine's father from being run down by an auto, and thus meets the heroine, who was waiting for her father and has witnessed the rescue.

The heroine and a friend of the hero (who is using the hero's name) are married by mistake in a French village, so the heroine's first meeting with the hero is in the rôle of a wife whom he has unknowingly married by proxy.

The heroine is a popular evangelist and first meets the hero when he answers her call for volunteers to demonstrate their "faith" by entering a lion's cage on the stage of the tabernacle.

The hero is among the audience in a café where the heroine is an entertainer. He smiles at her and she tosses him a rose, then later, when she is passing among the crowd, slips him the key to her living quarters.

The heroine, a Russian princess, is stopping at an inn where the hero and his robber band also stop. She and her friend hear the hero singing, and, at their request, he comes to their room to sing for them.

The hero is standing sentry duty on a ship when the captain's daughter, the heroine, passes by. The sea is very rough, and as she is struggling for a footing, she is catapulted into his arms.

The hero is a magician, and the heroine is the sister of his assistant, a young boy whom he picked up on the street suffering from amnesia and whose identity he has been trying to discover. The heroine comes to a performance at the theater to try to identify her brother and thus meets the hero.

The hero, a wealthy meat-packer with two young sons, meets the heroine when she comes to his house as an entertainer at the unveiling of a statue purchased by one of his sons. She meets him on the doorstep, where he has been refused entrance by a new butler who does not recognize him, and the heroine is pleasant to him. The hero enters the house and is preparing for bed in his own room when the heroine, mistaking it for her dressing room, enters and commences to dress for her appearance as an entertainer.

It is evident that the motion picture emphasizes the unusual, that there is here an essential lack of realism, that it involves a Cinderella conception of acquaintanceship. Is this desirable? Does it tend to rob immature youth of an insight into the real nature of the situations under which men and women live? Does it induce a type of phantasy-building which thwarts the emotional maturing of the individual? These questions are not answered by the data.

We may inquire, however, whether it is possible to build motion-picture drama without these unusual types of meeting which bulk so large in the movie fare. Do we need this emphasis on the unusual? The writer is inclined to believe that frequently the utilization of such unusual situations is an indication of a lack of skill on the part of scenario writers. Certainly it is more difficult to build up a dramatic situation where the characters are previously known and where they meet under ordinary circumstances than it is where they are unknown to one another and meet under unusual and extraordinary conditions.

Data have also been compiled on the degree of acquaint-

anceship of leading characters who are involved in love relationships. These are presented in Table 25.

We see from the table that 3 pictures had no love element.
In 14 of the remaining pictures, 14 of the heroes and heroines
were shown as falling in love immediately upon meeting. In
10 pictures love was shown as a matter of two or three
meetings. This, too, falls logically under the classification

TABLE 25

DEGREE OF ACQUAINTANCESHIP OF LEADING CHARACTERS INVOLVED IN
LOVE RELATIONSHIPS IN THE 40 PICTURES

Number and per cent of pictures in which each degree of acquaintanceship was shown

Degree of Acquaintanceship	Number	Per cent [a]
Love at first sight		
Extreme cases, immediate....................	14	35
A matter of two or three meetings...........	10	25
Love as a growth............................	2	5
Time element uncertain......................	3	7.5
Engaged when picture opens.................	5	12.5
Story of married life........................	10	25
No love element.............................	3	7.5

[a] This total exceeds 100 per cent because of the fact that more than one pair of
characters per picture is tabulated, thereby occasionally placing a picture in more
than one category.

of love at first sight. In other words, in 24 pictures we saw
the hero and heroine falling in love either on first acquaint-
ance or shortly thereafter. In 5 pictures the characters are
shown as engaged when the play begins. Ten of the pictures
are stories of married life, and this will be described in
Chapter VII. In only 2 of the pictures was love clearly shown
as a slow growth.

Some persons may not be inclined to look upon these data
with any great degree of seriousness. They may feel that
after all these are merely movie patterns and that no one

believes that they are taken seriously by those who view them. Such statements usually come from sophisticated persons who view motion-picture drama either with a certain amount of scorn or with a liberal sprinkling of adult discount. However, when we consider the millions of adolescents and young folk who are in large measure "emotionally possessed" by these motion pictures, we must realize that for many of them these patterns of life are very real. The reader, therefore, is asked to consider the above data in the light of the following statement by Mrs. Walter Ferguson:

> The romantic ideal, with its sentimental stickiness, fostered by moving pictures, popular magazines, newspaper serials, remains a perpetual barrier to any sane common-sense working-out of our marriage problems. For it promotes the idea that without preparation, without unselfishness, without a congeniality of tastes, a man and woman can remain happily married on passion.
>
> . . . .
>
> These romantic stories are very pretty so long as we regard them as entertainment, but once we believe that they are models after which life should be patterned we are lost.[1]

LOVEMAKING

Many students of the motion picture have pointed out the influence of the cinema on behavior patterns. They have repeatedly indicated that the motion picture has had a tremendous effect on patterns of lovemaking. Our analysis of these love scenes has been carried forward in order to secure an answer to the following questions:

1. Who are the characters involved in the lovemaking?
2. Under what circumstances do the leading characters in motion pictures make love?
3. What are the specific techniques of lovemaking emphasized?
4. Where do they make love?

[1] "A Woman's Viewpoint," *Columbus Citizen*, February 1, 1933.

An attempt to classify the content of motion pictures on the basis of the lovemaking contained therein involves many difficulties. In the first place, one who is trying to classify lovemaking merely on the basis of the particular scenes in which it occurs is likely to fall into serious error, since the context of that lovemaking is extremely important. A certain situation which, on the face of it, may not appear to represent intense emotion will, if the circumstances surrounding that lovemaking are known, be considered a very tense situation.

It is evident, for example, that if the intense lovemaking opened the picture, its effect on the observer would not be nearly so great as if it were properly built up with a number of scenes preceding it. Indeed, the writer is inclined to believe that certain scenes, if built up in different ways, would be described by observers as offensive or inoffensive, depending in great measure upon the scenes which precede them. If, for example, we know that the heroine is married but is carrying on an affair with another man, her love scenes with the other man would take on much more intensity than if this same lovemaking were shown with her husband. In other words, the context that is set up for the scene influences our decision regarding its attractiveness or unattractiveness, its intensity or lack of it.

Specific statements of the nature of the intense, moderate, and friendly types of lovemaking are presented in order to indicate the meaning of these three categories:

Examples of Intense Lovemaking
    Toby, a married man, roughly kisses a young flapper who has taunted him.
    A young man sits down on the bed and puts his arms about his wife and kisses her warmly. She puts her hands against his face.

Babka lies down on the couch with Grischa. They kiss long and ardently and suddenly Grischa seems to come to himself and says, "No, no, Babka! It wasn't for this I gave the Germans the slip! I must be on my way again."

Hank, a humorous character, follows the Queen to her couch. He gingerly puts his arms about her; she turns and gives him a passionate kiss; whereupon Hank blushes furiously and falters, "But—but, Queenie—my intentions are honorable!" He then places his arms about her and bends her back until she is leaning halfway to the floor.

The wife of a newspaper editor has a clandestine meeting with a banker. She professes her love for him and her voice is smothered as their lips meet and they embrace closely.

When the hero gingerly takes a seat beside the heroine, she pulls his face down to her and holds him closely. Later she undresses and is wearing a transparent silk and lace nightgown with a thin negligee over it. She stretches herself out luxuriously and inquires of him how she looks. He replies, "Like one hundred and ten pounds of dynamite." She then orders him to sit down beside her on the couch, and as he seats himself uneasily, she stretches, then puts her hands about his shoulders and pulls him down toward her.

Examples of Moderate Lovemaking

Tom, the hero, holds Lou's hands, then takes her into his arms.

The heroine turns and puts her arms around the hero as he drops his head broken-heartedly. "Oh, it's all right, John," she assures him tenderly, kissing him on the cheek.

When the Colonel asks the heroine if she loves him, she answers, "More every day." He puts his arm about her and she leans her cheek against his shoulder.

The hero kisses the heroine hurriedly and she goes into the house.

Jack tells Helen that he loves her and he has always loved her, and then goes to her and puts his arms about her.

Examples of Friendly or Affectionate Lovemaking

Gemma goes back to join the guests and on the way passes Ronnie, who silently clasps her hand for a second.

The villain sits down beside the heroine and pats her hand sympathetically.

The heroine and Jimmy run up the steps together, his arm about her waist.

Bradon takes her by the shoulders. She turns around reluctantly, but as he pats her on the arm, begs him to let her go.

Amy turns and runs back to Bessiere, where she impulsively puts both arms about his neck, kisses his hand hastily, then again hurries back.

Table 26 presents not only the percentages of the various types of lovemaking but also the characters involved. It will be noted, as would be expected, that the hero and heroine

TABLE 26

LEADING CHARACTERS INVOLVED IN LOVEMAKING IN THE 40 PICTURES

Distribution of characters involved in lovemaking according to number of pictures, number and per cent of occurrences, and degree of intensity

Type of Character	Per cent of Occurrences	Number of Occurrences				Number of Pictures
		Type of Lovemaking			Total	
		Intense	Moderate	Friendly		
Hero and heroine......	55	58	43	21	122	34
Man and woman......	16	2	20	14	36	15
Man and heroine......	11	2	10	12	24	14
Hero and woman......	6	2	6	6	14	8
Villain and heroine.....	6	3	5	5	13	6
Man and villainess.....	3	1	3	2	6	3
Hero and villainess.....	2	3	1	1	5	4
Villain and woman.....			1		1	1
Villain and villainess...				1	1	1
Number of occurrences .		71	89	62	222	
Per cent of occurrences .		32	40	28	100	
Number of pictures....		28	31	29		36
Per cent of pictures....		70	78	73		90

are responsible for the majority of the lovemaking scenes. They are found making love in 34 of the 40 pictures, and they account for 58 of the 71 cases of intense lovemaking,

43 of the 89 cases of moderate lovemaking, and only 21 of the 62 cases of friendly lovemaking.

These data are summarized still further in Table 27. It will be noted that the villain makes love in only 15 scenes of the total 222, and in 13 of these scenes he is making love to the heroine.

TABLE 27

FREQUENCY OF LOVEMAKING BY EACH TYPE OF CHARACTER IN THE 40 PICTURES

Number and per cent of occurrences of lovemaking by each type of character

Type of Character	Heroine	Woman	Villain-ess	Total Occurrences	
				Number	Per cent
Hero..................	122	14	5	141	63
Man..................	24	36	6	66	30
Villain...............	13	1	1	15	7
Number of occurrences..	159	51	12	222	
Per cent of occurrences..	72	23	5	100	

The second question is: Under what circumstances do the leading characters in motion pictures make love? Table 28 offers us information on this point.

The table is read as follows: The making of love under general circumstances is found in 23 pictures. (Under this category we have placed all those scenes of lovemaking which appear to arise from no specific cause.) These 23 pictures have 4 scenes of intense lovemaking, 22 of moderate love-making, and 20 of friendly lovemaking. This makes a total of 46 scenes involving lovemaking under what we have called *general circumstances*, and this includes 21 per cent of the occurrences.

The declaration of love accounts for the next highest total of scenes of lovemaking, 34 of them, or 15 per cent, being of this type. It may be noted further that declaration of love is found in 26 pictures. These in turn are followed, in order of total scenes, by lovemaking under the circumstances of meeting, parting, reconciliation, advances, gratitude, pro-

TABLE 28

CIRCUMSTANCES UNDER WHICH LOVEMAKING TOOK PLACE IN THE 40 PICTURES

Distribution of circumstances of lovemaking according to number of pictures, number and per cent of occurrences, and degree of intensity

Circumstance	Per cent of Occur- rences	Number of Occurrences				Number of Pictures
		Type of Lovemaking			Total	
		Intense	Mod- erate	Friendly		
General.............	21	4	22	20	46	23
Declaration of love.....	15	21	13	0	34	26
Meeting.............	13	9	14	5	28	21
Parting.............	12	5	17	4	26	19
Reconciliation........	9	12	6	1	19	12
Advances...........	8	2	7	8	17	12
Gratitude...........	7	1	4	10	15	11
Proposal of marriage...	5	8	0	3	11	10
Exultation...........	3	4	2	1	7	6
Sympathy...........	3	0	2	4	6	6
Wheedling...........	2	0	1	4	5	5
To arouse jealousy.....	1	0	1	1	2	2
To trap a man........	1	1	0	1	2	1
Appearances.........	1	2	0	0	2	1
Anger..............	0	1	0	0	1	1
Collect bet...........	0	1	0	0	1	1
Number of occurrences.		71	89	62	222	
Per cent of occurrences.		32	40	28	100	
Number of pictures....		28	31	29		36
Per cent of pictures....		70	78	73		90

posal of marriage, exultation, sympathy, wheedling, to arouse jealousy, to trap a man, for appearances, through anger, and to collect a bet.

We discover further that lovemaking occurs in 36 of the 40 pictures, or 90 per cent.

The reader will also be interested in the relationship between the intense, moderate, and friendly types of love-making. It will be noted that intense lovemaking appears in 28 of the 40 pictures, or 70 per cent. Further, there are 71 cases of intense lovemaking in 28 pictures, an average of less than 3 per picture. The intense lovemaking occurs most frequently in the declaration of love, and in reconciliation.

Moderate lovemaking occurs in 31 of the pictures, or 78 per cent. There is a total of 89 cases of moderate lovemaking, or slightly less than 3 per picture.

Friendly lovemaking occurs in 29 of the pictures, or 73 per cent. There are 62 cases of friendly lovemaking, or slightly more than 2 per picture.

There was a total of 222 different cases of lovemaking, or an average of more than 5 per picture. However, since there were 4 pictures in which no lovemaking at all occurred it will be noted that in 36 pictures there were an average of slightly more than 6 lovemaking scenes in each picture.

An examination of the circumstances under which love-making takes place shows a great variety. (The movie lovemaking curriculum is a broad one.) It is evident, there-fore, that the viewer of these pictures will get a good deal of information concerning techniques of lovemaking in a va-riety of typical situations. The reader may be interested in a description of some of the situations under which love-making takes place. The circumstances surrounding a proposal of marriage may be of interest. How do the leading characters propose marriage? Descriptions of methods of marriage proposal follow:

> The Colonel and the heroine are preparing a meal. He sug-gests that the heroine and her sister come with him to Arizona and says, "You see, she could live with us—if we were mar-ried."
>
> He puts his hands on her shoulders, and as she turns around

in surprise, takes her in his arms. "Why, Frank—" she exclaims, "you're proposing to me."

The hero has just met the heroine a few hours before. When he asks her whether she is in love with anyone now, she replies, "No." He then informs her, "You will be—you've got to be—because I've decided that you and I are going to get married."

The hero tells his defeated rival, "You're going ashore with us." He then links his arm through his sweetheart's and continues, "You're going to be best man."

The hero tells the heroine, whose name he does not know, that they aren't going to leave until it is decided whether her name is to be Henderson or not. She laughs and says, "That has the earmarks of a proposal."

"It's nothing else but," he agrees. "I'm asking you to marry me, and I'm not going to stop asking you until you say 'yes.'"

The scout says to the heroine, "I'm askin' you a question and the answer can't be maybe. It's got to be yes or no—straight out—understand? Will you marry me—yes or no?"

"Oui, Monsieur," she replies naughtily. "Oui, oui, Monsieur." Then, laughing at his puzzled expression, she throws her arms about him and exclaims, "Yes!"

Leach, a humorous character, takes Angela in his arms and is making love to her in a very melodramatic fashion. He asks her to marry him; she shyly consents; and he becomes delirious with joy.

The hero points out to the heroine the falsity and inadequacy of the type of life she is living with her husband. He tells her that he is leaving in a few days for Paris, telling her that he loves her, and asks her to come with him, the inference being that she should divorce her present husband and marry the hero.

It is evident that marriage proposals in these 40 motion pictures have a type of sanity and sophistication about them that is quite wholesome.

Only one picture showed a proposal of marriage by letter:

The hero has written to the heroine, saying that the next time he sees her in negligee, he hopes that it will not be through a window but—through a church. And adds, "I hope to kiss your hand in fact as I do now in fancy."

Information concerning the techniques of lovemaking is presented in Table 29. A kiss and embrace is the most common technique used. In 63 of the cases it is considered intense lovemaking, in 23 it is moderate, and in 2 it is friendly. Further, there are 88 different scenes of kissing and embracing, and these comprise 40 per cent of the total scenes of lovemaking.

TABLE 29

TECHNIQUES OF LOVEMAKING USED IN THE 40 PICTURES

Distribution of lovemaking techniques according to number of pictures, number and per cent of occurrences and degree of intensity

| Technique | Per cent of Occurrences | Number of Occurrences | | | | Number of Pictures |
| | | Type of Lovemaking | | | Total | |
		Intense	Moderate	Friendly		
Kiss and embrace......	40	63	23	2	88	31
Embrace.............	22	6	28	16	50	26
Kiss................	16	2	28	5	35	19
Caress..............	8		1	16	17	12
Taking—Holding hands	7			15	15	13
Kissing hand..........	4		5	3	8	6
Carrying woman.......	2		4	1	5	5
Throwing kiss.........	2			4	4	4
Number of occurrences..		71	89	62	222	
Per cent of occurrences..		32	40	28	100	
Number of pictures....		28	31	29		36
Per cent of pictures....		70	78	73		90

A fourth question arises: Where do they make love? These data are presented in Table 30. It will be noted in 31 of the pictures, or slightly more than 75 per cent, that the viewers of these pictures will see lovemaking either in the living room (18 pictures) or in the bedroom (13 pictures).

TABLE 30

LOCATION OF LOVEMAKING IN THE 40 PICTURES

Distribution of locations of lovemaking according to number of pictures, number and per cent of occurrences, and degree of intensity

Location	Pictures		Occurrences				
	Number	Per cent	Type of Lovemaking			Total	
			Intense	Moderate	Friendly	Number	Per cent
Living room	18	45	15	18	7	40	18
Bedroom	13	33	11	8	3	22	10
Automobile	8	20	1	5	3	9	4
Outdoors (general)	7	18	5	8	1	14	6
Aboard ship	6	15	4	4	7	15	7
Café	6	15	1	1	5	7	3
Street	5	13	2	5	1	8	4
Room	5	13	1	1	4	6	3
Kitchen	5	13	2	2	1	5	2
Hall	4	10	3	4	2	9	4
Garden	4	10	1	2	3	6	3
Hotel—Inn	4	10	1	2	3	6	3
Drawing-room	4	10	1	1	3	5	2
Cabin	3	8	2	3	2	7	3
Ballroom	3	8	1	3	1	5	2
Boudoir	3	8	5			5	2
Theater	3	8	2	2	1	5	2
Dining—Breakfast room	3	8		3	1	4	2
House	3	8		3		3	1
Camp	2	5		2	2	4	2
Office	2	5	1	1	2	4	2
Hospital	2	5		1	2	3	1
Racetrack	2	5	1		2	3	1
Beach	2	5	1	1		2	1
Castle—Palace	2	5	1	1		2	1
Library	2	5	1		1	2	1
Roof garden	2	5		2		2	1
Saloon	2	5		2		2	1
Woods	2	5	2			2	1
Veranda—Porch	1	3	1		1	2	1
Aboard airplane	1	3	1			1	
Aboard train	1	3		1		1	
Classroom—Schoolroom	1	3			1	1	
Desert	1	3	1			1	
Football field	1	3			1	1	
Grandstand	1	3			1	1	
Hack	1	3			1	1	
Jail—Prison	1	3		1		1	
Locker room—Dressing room	1	3	1			1	
Military headquarters	1	3	1			1	
Road	1	3		1		1	
Seacoast	1	3	1			1	
Studio	1	3		1		1	
Number of occurrences			71	89	62	222	
Per cent of occurrences			32	40	28		100
Number of pictures	36		28	31	29		
Per cent of pictures		90	70	78	73		

99

This involves a total of 62 scenes and comprises 28 per cent of the entire group of 222 lovemaking situations.

The reader may be interested to note that in 8 of the 40 pictures, lovemaking is shown in an automobile. Furthermore, out of the total of 42 different settings which serve as a location for lovemaking, 27, or approximately two thirds, are interior settings. And when we examine the 12 most frequent locations of lovemaking, we discover that only 3 are exterior settings.

SUMMARY

The study of the circumstances of meeting and nature of lovemaking was based on the 40 pictures which were intensively analyzed. Only the *heroes* and *heroines* involved in love relationships were tabulated in regard to acquaintanceship. In 1 picture there was no *heroine*, in 13 pictures the *hero* and *heroine* were acquainted prior to the opening of the picture, in 9 they meet in a usual situation, and in 17 in an unusual situation. In 11 pictures they are shown as being introduced and in 15 they are not.

The degree of acquaintanceship of characters involved in love relationships was as follows: In only 5 per cent of the pictures was romantic love shown as a slow growth; 60 per cent showed love as either at first sight or as a matter of two or three meetings. The remaining pictures either dealt with a type of love in which the time element was uncertain, or the characters were engaged when the picture opened, or it was a story of married life. Seven and a half per cent showed no love element.

Three types of lovemaking—*intense, moderate*, and *friendly*—were defined. *Moderate* lovemaking was shown in 78 per cent of the pictures while *friendly* and *intense* were seen respectively in 73 and 70 per cent of the pictures. The major portion of the lovemaking is done by the *hero* and *heroine*.

Sixteen circumstances of lovemaking were shown. The first in rank was that classified as *general,* followed by *declaration of love, meeting, parting,* and *reconciliation.* It is interesting to note that *proposal of marriage* as a circumstance of lovemaking ranks eighth and is shown in 5 per cent of the occurrences.

Eight techniques of lovemaking were shown. The *kiss and embrace* was by far the most common technique.

Forty-two types of settings served as a background for lovemaking. The majority of these were interior sets. Lovemaking occurred most frequently in the living room, being seen almost twice as often as in the next most common location, the bedroom.

Have the movies improved on the old fairy tale pattern of love and romance? Love at first sight persists and the unusual surrounds the circumstances of meeting. This is not much better than the old fairy tale. It would undoubtedly take a great deal of skill to present dramatically the average life love affair. It has been done in literature. It could be done in the movie. Would not such a presentation be desirable? Would it not enrich and enhance the experience of youth?

The question of lovemaking is a difficult one when considered in the light of the vast audience of adolescents. Lovemaking is an art in which practically every one needs to be skilled. It is a subject which does not lend itself well to verbal instruction. Therefore, the movies may be a logical agency to assume the responsibility for presenting this type of information. On the other hand, the viewing of intense love scenes may be exciting to unstable youth. Other studies in this series have shown that sexual delinquency sometimes follows motion pictures in which lovemaking played a major part. Perhaps the viewing of motion pictures develops in some youths an immunity to emotional excitement that is desirable.

The answers to these problems probably do not lie in terms of lovemaking or no lovemaking but in terms of how much. Intense lovemaking in almost 3 out of 4 pictures may be too high an average for most adolescents. The data probably point to the desirability of careful selection of the pictures to be seen.

CHAPTER VII

SEX, MARRIAGE, AND ROMANTIC LOVE

A SERIES of critical questions has arisen concerning sex, marriage, and love in the movies. These questions may be stated as follows:

1. What rôle should the motion picture play in setting up desirable standards in the field of sex, marriage, and love?
2. What proportion of the total number of pictures deal with sex, with love, with problems of marriage?
3. In what degree is violation of the current moral code shown in motion pictures as desirable or attractive?
4. What ideals of marriage are presented in the motion pictures which were studied?

What rôle should the motion picture play in setting up desirable standards in the field of sex, marriage, and love?

The tremendous value of drama in a changing civilization cannot be overestimated. Through drama, individuals who are concerned with the possible consequences of certain types of decision can obtain exact information about the effects of certain choices. They can obtain this information without the disastrous effects which sometimes accrue to those who personally discover the social consequences of experimentation in various fields of conduct. For many persons, therefore, drama represents a rehearsal of certain lines of conduct in which they are interested. It is a form of thinking, a mental experiment with varied choices.

It is for such reasons as these that the social consequences of certain choices made by leading characters in motion picturés in reference to sex, marriage, and love become especially important. If the production of our motion-picture drama is in the hands of persons who tend to think in a certain direction concerning these problems, then they will unconsciously or consciously influence their audiences to make similar decisions. There is need, therefore, for dramatists with artistic integrity, who can present the social consequences of certain choices with accuracy and clarity, since the pattern followed by the movie characters in regard to their important decisions may be followed by literally hundreds of thousands of people who view the films. We must never forget that the decisions made by the cinema characters in regard to any important problems of life at once become data in the thinking of millions of children, youth, and adults.

But we cannot remove bias. Human beings are fallible because they are human beings, and they are unable to survey all of the evidence impartially. What we need, therefore, is a sufficient diversity of treatment so that varying points of view can be presented as honestly as the dramatist knows how to present them.

Whether we will it or not, therefore, the motion picture gives us an education. It is an education in the consequences which may follow the making of certain choices and judgments. Where these consequences represent the responses of the mass of the audience, their portrayal serves to reënforce the mores of the group. When those choices are those which do not express the views of the mass of viewers, they may tend to cause them to review the wisdom of their previous decisions in particular areas of conduct. Society needs both types of films.

What proportion of the total number of pictures deals with sex, with love, with problems of marriage?

That many patterns of love behavior are shown in motion pictures is evidenced by these facts: In 1920, 44.6 per cent of the 500 pictures analyzed dealt with love as their principal theme. In 1925, 32.8 per cent dealt with this topic, and in 1930, 29.6 per cent were labeled as love pictures. (See Chapter II, page 17.) We have also shown that love-making occurs in 90 per cent of the 40 pictures which we analyzed in detail. Further, as we shall show in Chapter XI, the most common individual goal was *winning another's love* and the most common personal goal was *happiness of a loved one.*

In the 40 pictures which we analyzed in detail 10 of them presented some problem of married life, either as a major or

TABLE 31

Type of Character Having Illicit Love as a Major Goal in the 115 Pictures

The number of each type of character who had illicit love as a major goal

Type of Character	Number
Hero	4
Heroine	3
Villain	11
Villainess	7
Other men	7
Other women	3
Total	35

a minor theme. The specific problems presented will be found in a later discussion in this chapter.

The proportion of sex pictures in 500 movies in 1920 was 13 per cent, in 1925 it was 17 per cent, and in 1930 it was 15 per cent. We can conclude, then, that sex pictures as we have defined them (see Chapter II) have not appreciably increased or decreased in amount since 1920. The chances are, therefore, about one in seven that a child or adult who exercises no choice whatsoever in his selection of motion pictures will see a sex picture.

We can also repeat here evidence which will be more completely presented in Chapter XI. In 22 out of 115 pictures, illicit love was shown as a goal of 35 leading characters. The goals were distributed as shown in Table 31.

Illicit love was sixth in rank of the individual goals, being exceeded only by *winning another's love, marriage for love, professional success, revenge,* and *crime for gain.* These facts are sufficient to establish the truth of the statement that a significant proportion of the movies deal with the theme of illicit love.

Is this too high a proportion for children, for youth, for adults? We are unable adequately to answer this inquiry, but the material presented in the rest of this chapter may help the reader to think this question through. The following quotation from the *Hollywood Spectator*, written by its editor, Welford Beaton, sheds some light on the problem of overemphasis. Lest the reader think from the tone of this article that Mr. Beaton is a "reformer," an advocate of blue laws, and a general grouch, we merely state that he is not only one of the ablest screen critics, but he is also a personal friend of many of the screen luminaries. Further, the preface to his recent book, *Know Your Movies*, was written by Cecil B. DeMille. Mr. Beaton says:

When I was a youth, and even after I was old enough to vote, I liked to drink milk. A score or more years ago I had typhoid fever. During my hungry convalescence I looked forward to my periodical glass of milk, the sole article on my diet chart. Once I reached for it eagerly—but I could not drink it. At that moment the point of repulsion had been reached. Not since then have I drunk a drop of milk. The thought of it nauseates me. I do not watch anyone else drinking it.

The other day I was watching with keen appreciation of its many artistic qualities *The Easiest Way*, Constance Bennett's latest starring vehicle, produced by Metro. For the second time in my life there was an exact moment when the point of repulsion was reached. I had had enough sex. I want no more of it in my screen entertainment. . . .

The makers of our screen entertainment may continue to earn dividends by selling the immorality of women, but no longer can they sell it to me. I serve notice that every sex picture that I review from now on is going to be estimated for what it is— a filthy thing manufactured by business men. . . .[1]

I think no one would maintain that pre-adolescent children should be permitted to see sex pictures. We need not even argue the question of probable harm. Even though no harm were to result, the time spent viewing such pictures might be much better spent in some other fashion.

For youth, however, the case is not so clear. Most intelligent parents would not want to keep their adolescent boys and girls uninformed about important sex problems. And it is manifestly true that some of these sex problems are best presented in dramatic form, either in legitimate drama or in motion pictures. Whether the motion-picture producers at present are capable of performing this delicate task satisfactorily is a debatable problem.

Among enlightened parents, therefore, there will be no objection to the presentation to youth of sex drama, but these parents wish to set up at least three standards for such drama. First, the problems should be of a type which faces the group which is to see them. Second, the viewers ought to be given all the pertinent facts in the situation. Third, the material ought to be deftly handled by a creative artist.

In what degree is violation of the current moral code shown in motion pictures as desirable or attractive?

[1] *Hollywood Spectator*, February 28, 1931, p. 3.

One of the most dangerous aspects of this situation in
reference to motion pictures is that colorful and attractive
stars are commonly given rôles depicting women who lose
their virtue, who are ruined by men, lead profligate lives.
Perhaps Dan Thomas, a Hollywood writer for the Newspaper
Enterprise Association Service, can tell this story better than
the writer. He says:

> What has happened to the old-fashioned screen vamp? And,
> at the same time, one might ask the question regarding the
> innocent young leading lady. Both seem to have passed out of
> the picture about the same time, to be replaced by our modern
> leading lady with all the sweetness and charm of a Marguerite
> Clark combined with the more or less loose morals of a Theda
> Bara.
>
> Just what brought about this change seems to be a bit uncer-
> tain. But one thing is quite definite—the new arrangement
> apparently followed a new trend as set by real persons rather
> than the public at large patterning themselves after reel charac-
> ters. The day has passed when a man will fall for the obvious
> gestures of the old-fashioned vamp. Neither is he interested in
> the naïve girlish type. Still, a girl is not considered exactly bad
> these days even though her morals are a bit loose as long as she
> is discreet in her actions.
>
> Consequently, the Theda Baras, Nazimovas, Barbara La
> Marrs, May Allisons, Marguerite Clarks and Lillian Gishes have
> disappeared from the screen. And in their places we find Greta
> Garbo, Norma Shearer, Marlene Dietrich, Tallulah Bankhead,
> Joan Crawford, Constance Bennett, Carole Lombard, Claudette
> Colbert, Jean Harlow, Karen Morley, Ann Dvorak and others.
>
> Throughout her entire career Garbo has at least touched on
> the shady side of life. I can't recall a single film in which she
> portrayed what might be regarded as a good woman. Right at
> the start we found her drinking the dregs in "The Torrent"
> and in "Grand Hotel" new life came to her when she found a
> new lover.
>
> During some years on the screen Norma Shearer's success
> was only mediocre until she came along as the reckless girl in

"Divorcee." In every film since then—"Strangers May Kiss,"
"A Free Soul," "Private Lives," and now "Strange Interlude"
—she has been ravishing and revealing, almost a torch bearer
for the single standard. And the fans have flocked into her camp.

Marlene Dietrich never had a chance to go straight in films
in this country. She lost that chance by making such a hit as
the "bad" dancer in "Blue Angel," the German-made film
which resulted in her present contract. Since then she has made
"Morocco," "Dishonored," and "Shanghai Express," portraying the same type of character in each.

Perhaps the secret of Tallulah Bankhead's success on the
screen can be attributed to the rather loose but still charming
women she has portrayed. She has yet to appear in a single
production which could be stamped as first class. But with her
three poor films she managed to build up a tremendous following.

Joan Crawford started out to be a shady lady in her first film,
"Sally, Irene and Mary." However, virtue still was a premium
in those days so Joan met with disaster while the hero and
heroine went into their usual clinch in the final reel. However,
both the hero and heroine of that picture long since have been
forgotten while Joan has gone merrily on her way to dizzy
heights.

Connie Bennett is another who has found that it doesn't pay
to be good—at least not on the screen. Since her return to films
about two years ago Connie has tasted nothing but success.
Her slightest wish has been granted. And Connie certainly isn't
a goody-goody.

Then there's Jean Harlow. Jean never has had what might
be termed an outstanding picture, except "Hell's Angels," in
which she had only a minor rôle. But she always has played a
good-bad girl. And she is doing very nicely these days.

And so it goes. Practically the same thing can be said for
almost every one of our younger actresses who are getting along
these days. Virtue may have been a premium once—but apparently it slumped along with other leading stocks.[2]

Again, we must note that this is written not by some one
who "has it in for the movies." On the contrary, I repeat

[2] *Berkshire County Eagle*, Pittsfield, Mass., July 13, 1932,

that it is written by a reporter who covers motion-picture
events for the Newspaper Enterprise Association Service.

Further, it must be pointed out that there is no diminu-
tion, so far as the writer can determine, in the number of
pictures dealing with this theme. As evidence he cites the
following sex pictures, produced in 1932 and 1933. No attempt was made to obtain an exhaustive list. They are
sufficient in number, however, to make the reader realize
that the emphasis on sex in motion pictures is still with us.

"Strange Interlude"—Tells the story of a married woman
who has a child by her best friend because she fears the taint
of insanity in her husband.

"Animal Kingdom"—The hero finds that his mistress is more
truly his wife than the woman he married. He reminiscently
points out that his wife resembles the prostitutes with whom he
used to consort abroad.

"Cynara"—Develops the problem of a husband's infidelity
and its effect upon his life.

"Rasputin and the Empress"—Includes the seduction by
Rasputin of one of the ladies in waiting.

"State Fair"—From the book of that name, cuts down the
book's two seductions to one, and realistically presents the bed
and bedroom in which the lovers are lying.

"She Done Him Wrong"—Concerns itself mainly with the
career of a famous prostitute, including her attempts to seduce a
young religious worker.

"Farewell to Arms"—Deals realistically with a seduction of
a nurse by a soldier.

"Child of Manhattan"—The hero, the son of a wealthy man,
marries the heroine when he discovers that she is about to have a
child.

"Topaze"—One of the characters has as his mistress the leading woman character.

"Flesh"—Wallace Beery marries the heroine, who later gives
birth to a child fathered by a former lover.

"If I Had a Million"—In one of the stories in this unique play, the method which a prostitute used to spend her million is outlined.

We turn now to another question: What ideals of marriage are presented in the motion pictures which were studied?

I think we are safe in saying that the motion pictures constitute an important source of such ideals. If this is true, then the patterns of marriage behavior shown in motion pictures ought to be carefully scrutinized for the lessons which they teach. We need to learn of the circumstances under which persons meet and plan their marriage. We need to know the ages at which these characters are married. We need to learn the nature of the wedding ceremony. We need to learn how married couples solve the difficulties normally faced in this new situation. We need to discover the criterion of married success set up in these motion-picture stories.

Evidence on a number of these points has been obtained. In some cases the evidence is very detailed and clear-cut, but at other points it is inadequate.

MARITAL STATUS

The marital status of the leading characters often gives many clues as to the type of content of the picture. If a large proportion of the heroes and heroines are unmarried, we may expect that such pictures will concern themselves in large measure with romance and lovemaking. If, on the other hand, we find that most of the heroes and heroines are married, we can logically expect that such pictures will deal with problems of married life or with divorce.

Here are the facts about the marital status of the heroes, heroines, villains, and villainesses in the 40 pictures studied in detail:

Thirty-two of the 39 heroes were unmarried at the beginning of the picture. Six were married during the picture.

Thirty of the 39 heroines were unmarried at the beginning of the picture. Five were married during the picture. One was divorced and then remarried.

Seventeen of the 30 villains and 4 of the 7 villainesses were unmarried at the beginning of the picture. None was married during the picture.

We also have data on all the leading characters in these 40 pictures, since the above data deal only with heroes, heroines, villains, and villainesses. These have been compared in Table 32 with the United States Census data for 1930 relative to the per cent of the population of the United States over the age of 15 that was single, married, or widowed.

TABLE 32

COMPARISON OF THE MARITAL STATUS OF THE LEADING CHARACTERS IN
THE 40 PICTURES WITH THE MARITAL STATUS OF THE UNITED
STATES POPULATION AS SHOWN BY THE 1930 CENSUS

Marital Status	Male		Female	
	Census Per cent	Movie Per cent[a]	Census Per cent	Movie Per cent
Single....................	34	66	26	71
Married..................	60	15	61	21
Widowed.................	5	2	12	7
Divorced.................	1		1	1

[a] It was impossible to determine the marital status of 17 per cent of the male leading characters.

One notes at once the striking discrepancies between the two sets of figures. Perhaps, however, we cannot reasonably expect that we would have the same proportions of characters single, married, widowed, and divorced as we have in the general population. Nevertheless, if the motion-picture audience is selected from people in all walks of life, young and old, married and unmarried, rich and poor, as we have so often been told by the motion-picture producers, we realize that what is presented on the screen may frequently miss entirely the interests and activities of vast portions of the audience.

Some might maintain, on the other hand, that romantic love of unmarried persons is an affair which greatly pleases all, whether married or unmarried. Perhaps this is true. Nevertheless, it is equally certain that motion-picture producers have not yet discovered how to make the romance of marriage as appealing and interesting on the screen as the romance of pre-marital life.

There are some data to indicate that younger persons, let us say under the age of 25, are more frequent attenders of motion pictures than those over this age. This is sometimes given as a reason why we so frequently have a story which deals with the activities of unmarried persons. If this is true, it may merely be an indication of the lack of perspicacity on the part of the producer in failing to develop motion pictures of married life which will appeal strongly to persons beyond the age of 25.

Further, in view of the great complexity of marriage and the inadequate training of our youth for this relationship, might it not well be the function of the motion picture to portray the activities that go to make up a well-balanced and satisfactory married life? Surely we can as reasonably expect young unmarried people to be just as interested in a picture of married life as we can expect those who are married to enjoy a picture relating to the love and romance of unmarried folk.

CIRCUMSTANCES UNDER WHICH MARRIAGE TAKES PLACE

Marriages were shown as occurring in 11 of the 40 pictures analyzed in detail. The actual wedding ceremonies were shown in 6 of these pictures. Two of the weddings were large, formal affairs. There were also one military and one small wedding. These weddings included the religious ceremony. (Two of the pictures showed a wedding ceremony being performed by a civil official.) In 4 of the 40 pictures the marriage was the result of an elopement. In the fourth, elopement is shown as having harmful consequences, although in this picture the harmful consequences are not shown as directly related to the elopement.

In two cases the wedding was not shown but was merely suggested; in one case through statements of the characters, and in the other, through close-ups of clasped hands and wedding bells.

AGES OF MARRIED AND UNMARRIED LEADING CHARACTERS

What pattern does the motion picture set up as to the desirable age at which to be married?

TABLE 33

COMPARISON OF AGE WITH MARITAL STATUS OF THE LEADING CHARACTERS AT THE BEGINNING OF THE 40 PICTURES

The number and per cent of characters of each age group in each marital status. Only leading characters whose marital status was obvious were used

| Age Group | Marital Status | | | | | | | | | | | Total | |
| | Unmarried | | Married | | Divorced | | Remarried | | Widowed | | | | |
	No.	Per cent	No.	Per cent	No.	Per cent	No.	Per cent	No.	Per cent		No.	Per cent
1–5...........	1	100.0										1	100
6–13...........	2	100.0										2	100
14–18...........	8	100.0										8	100
19–22...........	23	100.0										23	100
23–26...........	30	76.9	7	18.0	1	2.6			1	2.6		39	100
27–30...........	27	79.4	6	17.7					1	2.9		34	100
31–35...........	17	81.0	4	19.1								21	100
36–40...........	13	65.0	6	30.0					1	5.0		20	100
41–45...........	6	75.0	1	12.5			1	12.5				8	100
46–50...........	1	16.7	4	66.7					1	16.7		6	100
51–55...........	2	22.2	4	44.4					3	33.3		9	100
56–60...........	3	60.0	1	20.0					1	20.0		5	100
61–70...........	1	100.0										1	100
Total...........	134	75.7	33	18.6	1	.6	1	.6	8	4.5		177	100

An examination of Tables 33 and 34 shows that with increasing age the characters tend not to be shown as unmarried.

TABLE 34

COMPARISON OF AGE WITH MARITAL STATUS OF THE LEADING CHARACTERS
AT THE END OF THE 40 PICTURES

The number and per cent of characters of each age group in each marital status. Only leading characters whose marital status was obvious were used

| Age Group | Marital Status | | | | | | | | | | | | Total | |
| | Un-married | | Married | | Divorced | | Re-married | | Widowed | | Killed or Died | | | |
	No.	Per cent	No.	Per cent	No.	Per cent	No.	Per cent	No.	Per cent	No.	Per cent	No.	Per cent
1–5.........	1	100.0											1	100
6–13........	2	100.0											2	100
14–18.......	6	75.0	2	25.0									8	100
19–22.......	19	82.6	4	17.4									23	100
23–26.......	27	69.2	8	20.5			1	2.6	1	2.6	2	5.1	39	100
27–30.......	17	50.0	12	35.3					1	2.9	4	11.8	34	100
31–35.......	14	66.7	1	4.8	1	4.8			1	4.8	4	19.1	21	100
36–40.......	11	55.0	5	25.0					1	5.0	3	15.0	20	100
41–45.......	4	50.0	2	25.0							2	25.0	8	100
46–50.......			4	66.7	1	16.7			1	16.7			6	100
51–55.......			3	33.3					4	44.4	2	22.2	9	100
56–60.......	3	60.0	1	20.0					1	20.0			5	100
61–70.......	1	100.0											1	100
Total........	105	59.3	42	23.7	2	1.1	1	.6	10	5.6	17	9.6	177	100

It should be pointed out that a character need not be classified only as married or unmarried, so that the two categories do not add up to 100 per cent. We may have classified him as divorced, widowed, and indeterminate. More of them fall into these categories in the upper age brackets.

Let us turn now to the question: What problems in marriage do the leading characters face?

This can perhaps be best shown through presenting a résumé of 10 of the 40 pictures which have some problem of married life as a major or minor theme. These résumés follow:

The heroine has been jilted by the hero, after evidently having lived with him. In spite, she marries an older man who has been like a father to the hero. The hero threatens to expose her past, but cannot hurt his older friend. The hero then secretly marries the heroine's younger sister, in spite of the opposition of the heroine. The heroine, not knowing that they are married, compromises the young man in order to break up the affair. Upon discovery of his marriage, she tries to clear the hero of her false charges. In so doing, she is forced to tell her husband about her past, and is forgiven by him.

A young chorus girl finds that a marriage for money deprives her of joy and happiness. She divorces her husband and marries a penniless musician.

A newspaper editor, madly in love with his wife, discovers that she has been carrying on an illicit affair with a banker who has become involved in a stock scandal. The editor has been most ruthless in his policy of printing "everything that's news," and even in this case publishes a statement from his wife, shoots the banker, surrenders to the police, and takes a life sentence to the penitentiary.

The heroine, formerly a gangster's mistress, falls in love with and marries a respectable young man, without disclosing her true name or her past. Her secret is revealed, however, when the gangster is arrested for murder and she is forced to visit him. Due to pressure from her husband's family, she voluntarily renounces him. She has a child, which she at first refuses to surrender to her husband's family. She finally gives the child up, however, and when her husband returns from Europe, where he has gone to forget her, he becomes reconciled with his wife.

The hero, who is one of a band of thieves, marries the heroine because he thinks she has money and because it is "the only way he can get her." He is involved in a robbery, escapes, and the heroine is held by the police for questioning. Her husband returns, gives himself up, serves his sentence, and returns to her at the end of two years.

The hero and heroine, a young married couple, live very

happily and simply until a high-pressure auto salesman sells them a big car. The resultant "keeping up with the Joneses" nearly wrecks their marriage. But the hero's employer, from whom he has embezzled money, forces him to live simply in order to repay the stolen funds. The hero finally is able to sell the big car; the employer relents and gives him another job; and all ends happily with the young couple expecting a baby.

A wealthy, middle-aged banker and his wife are on their way to Europe. He is carrying on an illicit love affair with a Swedish dancer, and his wife is very unhappy. The hero is instrumental in breaking up the affair between the banker and dancer. When she discovers that the banking firm has failed, the banker's wife places her personal fortune at her husband's disposal although he says they have nothing to worry about financially. Their relations become much happier. There is an attempt made on his life, and during his convalescence, he becomes more devoted to his wife. At the end of the picture, they decide to return the securities which he has taken from the banking firm, and start over again, with each other.

A wealthy American girl, who is married to an English lord, thinks he is ideal until she discovers that he has been carrying on an illicit love affair, even before their marriage. She threatens to divorce him, but finds that she cannot because the other woman is her own sister-in-law, with whom her brother is madly in love. She therefore starts leading a life of wild gaiety, not caring how much people talk about her. Her husband is killed in an auto wreck, while with her sister-in-law, and in order to save the other woman's reputation the heroine blackens her own and lets it be inferred that she is the one who has been "unfaithful."

Two reporters, a young man and a young woman, fall in love at first sight and are married. They face difficulties because of financial problems and the young man's jealousy, not only of his wife's professional success, but also of her friendship with a business associate.

The hero is an Army pilot who has broken many records, but who is obsessed with a desire for further fame and publicity. His wife is unhappy because she sees so little of him, and because of the continual risks which he takes. When he insists upon going on an exploration trip, she makes plans to divorce him. He meets with an accident, however, and when he returns to civilization after a spectacular rescue, they are happily reunited.

That these problems are far removed from those faced by the majority of our population seems a satisfactory inference to draw from these stories. If the major function of drama is to clarify the thinking of the individuals who view it, then motion pictures as judged by this sampling have been grossly inadequate in fulfilling their function.

Many, however, would clamor for another function of the picture of married romance, namely, that of escape. Indeed, the *Detroit Free Press* writes as follows on this topic:

> What normal people read, say, and like to hear about marriage is far different from the way they live it. People seek release from actuality when they turn to entertainment, they don't want their movies, books, or news stories to portray comfortable, humdrum marriages such as their own, they ask the vicarious enjoyment of exploring emotional extremes impossible to daily life.
>
> In this light the popularity of the four-times-married movie Lothario (whose celluloid adventures never fail to return the audience to normality with a reassuringly happy ending) is seen merely as a safety valve. When plays of successful home life, ideal husbands, and contented wives begin to pack the theaters with audiences to whom such an existence is personally out of reach, then indeed it will be time to believe that marriage has become intolerable.[3]

Perhaps escape is sometimes needed from the worries and problems that beset married life. However, frequent excursions into the field of unreality may unfit one wholly or in

[3] August 27, 1932.

part to face the problems that still remain unsolved when one leaves the motion-picture theater.

A number of other questions concerning the pattern of married life will occur to the reader of this report. He will be anxious to know the nature of the activities which married persons carry out together. He will want to know whether they talk and plan about their children, whether they go hiking and riding together. He will want to know the part that children play in their lives. He will look for evidences of planning in regard to financial or domestic affairs. Yes, he will look for all of these things, but unfortunately he will not find them. For example, in these ten pictures of married life there is only one baby. A baby is expected at the end of another picture.

Pictures involving definite financial problems faced by the husband and wife are found only twice. In two other pictures financial problems occur, but one of them relates to embezzling and the other relates to a wife who has married a rich husband. Another picture is very definitely concerned with the problem of competitive ostentation. This material, however, is presented by comic characters and some of the import of the problem is thereby lost.

Summary

The facts in this chapter are gathered from the study of the 1,500 pictures released during the years 1920, 1925, and 1930; from the 115 pictures which were actually viewed; and from the 40 of these which were selected for detailed study.

Love was shown to be a favorite general topic, though the percentage of such pictures has decreased since 1920. The number of pictures which deal with *sex* as a general theme is about half those dealing with *love*, and a slight increase is shown in the ten-year period. In the 115 pictures, *winning another's love* was the most common individual goal of the leading characters, and *illicit love* ranked sixth. The villain was the character most often seen as having *illicit love* for his chief goal. Lovemaking occurred in 90 per cent of the 40 pictures.

In the 40 pictures three fourths of the leading characters were unmarried at the beginning of the pictures. Marriages occurred in approximately one fourth of the pictures. Over one half of the unmarried leading characters at the end of the picture were under 26 years of age.

One fourth of the pictures presented the problems of married life but an examination of these problems proved that they were somewhat unusual. One half of these problems centered around illicit love before or after marriage. Children were shown in one of the 10 pictures of married life.

This chapter has shown again the emphasis put on problems of romantic love and the related fields of sex and marriage.

The social desirability of accurate, appropriate, and artistic sex pictures is one that cannot reasonably be questioned. It is largely a question of number and treatment. Is one out of seven too many? Illicit love was evidently not shown as an entirely approved goal, as it was the villain who most often pursued this goal. However it was also shown four times as the goal of the hero, and three times as that of the heroine.

There is practically no representation of the problems of the single person over the age of 30, and the problems of marriage are inadequately presented. Would it not be desirable to have both sides of the picture clearly presented? Would divorces be lessened if, before marriage, youth knew more of the problems it would encounter? Certainly any presentation of married life which does not devote some attention to problems incident to the raising of children is inadequate.

CHAPTER VIII

CRIME IN THE MOVIES

THE material in this chapter can best be presented as answers to a series of critical questions concerning the movies. In some cases the data secured to answer these questions make it possible to draw clear-cut inferences from the facts. At other points the data are not so easily interpreted and serve only to illustrate the difficulty of securing easy answers to complicated social questions. Perhaps the most critical question, and the one least susceptible of a categorical answer, is the following:

What crime pictures, if any, should be included in the motion-picture bill of fare?

This question has agitated the public mind for many years, and a series of arguments pro and con have been stated in reference to it. Perhaps the best argument for such motion pictures is the one presented by Will Hays when he says,

> The proper treatment of crime as a social fact or as a dramatic motive is the inalienable right of a free press, of free speech, and of an unshackled stage or screen.

This argument has been expanded along the following lines by other defenders of this right.

Crime pictures, they say, depict an important phase of contemporary life. Since crime is a critical problem today, it is as important that the average person know of the prevalence of crime as that he know how to read and write. Further, the crime problem cannot be blotted out merely by

121

closing one's eyes to it, neither can evil be eliminated by putting a veil over it.

To put a ban on motion pictures dealing with crime is socially dangerous, because an enlightened public is far more helpful in curbing vice than a public deliberately kept ignorant. Moreover, the exposure of vice through the movies is less dangerous than the tolerance of vice by an attempt to prohibit exposure. Keeping children off the streets is not always the best way to prevent accidents. Neither is keeping the knowledge of crime from them the best way to teach them how to cope with the crime problem when they become mature.

Finally, we can have no literature or drama without the portrayal of conflict and frequently this conflict may deal with some critical moral problem. Crime is an important moral problem which deserves a place in our literature and on the screen.

The replies to these arguments would be stated somewhat like this:

We agree wholly with the need for an unshackled screen, for the treatment of crime *as a social fact*. But that treatment, and the treatment of any social fact, demands proper emphasis. Unfortunately, however, the motion-picture screen has given an emphasis to crime and violence which would characterize an individual as abnormal if he were thus preoccupied. This preoccupation crowds out pictures dealing with other fundamental problems of living. It makes the screen almost barren of pictures of beauty, idealism, and imaginative charm. Further, while there can be no approval of a screen which entirely shuts off fundamental facts from the public, yet one can get these facts from a variety of other sources, and frequently in much better form. Therefore, while we have no desire to exclude the fundamental and adequate treatment of crime from the screen, we do wish to accord it the emphasis which it receives in the lives of normal, intelligent people.

Such an able motion-picture critic as Alexander Bakshy, of *The Nation*, could hardly be accused of suggesting that any medium of communication should shy away from crime as a social fact. He does, however, make this comment about crime in motion pictures:

> Gangsters and racketeers play so prominent a part in the American life of today that it would be little short of a miracle if their exploits were ignored by the movies. Nor are they. In fact, the number of films dealing with the underworld and its criminal activities is altogether too great.[1]

Further, "social facts" ought to be presented to those who bear the responsibility of rectifying them. The solution of the crime problem is by no means the problem of the estimated 11,000,000 children, thirteen years of age and under, who were attending the motion pictures weekly in 1929. If crime is to be justified as a social fact, why not include it in the grade- and high-school libraries in the same proportion as it appears in the movie fare? No educator has ever recommended such a procedure, and it does not appear likely that it will be recommended.

PROPORTION OF CRIME PICTURES IN THE MOVIES

What do the facts which we have gathered concerning motion pictures show about the emphasis on crime in the movies? The proportion of pictures having crime as their *major theme* is as follows:

When 500 motion pictures in each of the years 1920, 1925, and 1930 were analyzed for major themes, it was discovered

[1] Bakshy, Alexander, "The Underworld," *The Nation*, CXXXII (January 21, 1931), p. 80.

that crime pictures appeared in the following proportions: 1920, 24 per cent; 1925, 30 per cent; and 1930, 27 per cent (see Chapter II). It should be pointed out, of course, that these are only the pictures which have crime as a major theme. Many other pictures which were classed under mystery, war, love, and so on, will include crime.

Is this proportion of crime pictures too high? We must ask, "Too high for whom?" If children exercised no choice whatsoever in their selection of films, we could expect that one film in every four which they see would be a crime picture as we have defined it. Certainly this proportion available to children is much higher than the proportion of crime literature that is available to them. Further, the proportion of crime pictures intelligible to children is far greater than is the proportion of books intelligible to them having crime as a major theme. We must also consider the fact that educational agencies which in large measure control the books available to children have very wisely guided the tastes of the child into areas believed by adults to be wholesome. Unfortunately, however, the schools have exercised almost no guidance in teaching children the wise selection of motion pictures. Many parents are becoming aware of the dangers of unguided motion-picture attendance, and are attempting to develop in their children wise standards of motion-picture evaluation.

Intelligent people will doubtless differ as to remedies for this situation, and some may believe that the *status quo* is satisfactory. Certainly, however, the high percentage of crime pictures should lead those responsible for the attitudes of children and youth toward crime to a very careful assaying of the effects of crime pictures upon children. We do know through Dr. Thurstone's studies that attitudes toward crime can be changed through motion pictures. It would seem wise, therefore, that unless there was some definite assurance of a favorable residue from the viewing of specific motion pictures, it would be best to avoid them entirely as a form of unsupervised entertainment for children. Accompanying such restrictive measures should be a type of wise educational guidance which will eventually develop in the child adequate standards for evaluating such pictures without the assistance of parent or teacher.

How is the criminal portrayed in the movies?
One group maintains that the crimes and criminals selected for motion-picture portrayal are not typical, that the motion-picture producers select glamorous crimes and criminals, that the criminal is frequently shown as an admirable, attractive person. Spokesmen for the opposing point of view maintain stoutly that the criminal is invariably pictured as a lawless, unattractive fellow, one whose qualities would in no wise mark him as a person to be imitated.

There is only one wholly adequate way of settling this problem, and that is to secure from individuals their reaction to such criminals as they are portrayed on the screen. Such studies as are reported by Dr. Thurstone in a companion volume illustrate this technique. In the absence of such complete, first-hand studies we can examine the attractiveness of such characters as evaluated by a group of intelligent adults who followed a written description of the criminals in 40 pictures and classified them as attractive, unattractive, or neither. The following are examples of those classed as attractive by these adults:

> The hero is the leader of a band of outlaws who terrorize a whole region by their hold-ups and robberies. There is a price upon his head, but throughout the picture he is shown as a man of great physical courage, admired by his followers, generous,

fair, and clever. In a gun battle at the end of the picture he shoots the villain, who well deserves it, and is himself killed.

The hero, leader of a robber band, is a handsome and colorful person. At the beginning of the picture he is seen as joyous, happy-go-lucky, disarmingly self-satisfied, and kind and thoughtful to his mother and younger sister. The death of his sister, however, arouses in him a flaming hatred of the aristocracy and a desire for vengeance. He possesses great physical courage, and his men admire and respect him. The Russian costumes which he wears are becoming to him, and his singing voice is beautiful.

The hero is a notorious gambler who is wanted by the police as a witness in vice-probe charges. He attempts a robbery on board the liner upon which he has taken passage, but is not successful. He is depicted as good-looking, extremely well-dressed, pleasant and courteous, clever and courageous. References indicate that his past has been somewhat vivid, but there is thrown about it an aura of glamour.

A second group of motion-picture characters classified as attractive are those who have committed military crimes. Their descriptions follow:

The hero makes his escape from a prison camp, and is seized by the Germans as a spy. He is shown as a simple, homesick soldier, at times frankly afraid, always hating war and what it stands for, but in his death showing a fine sort of courage.

Both the hero and the heroine are engaged in espionage, which is shown as a glamorous and exciting occupation. The hero is jaunty, adventure-loving, self-confident, of great physical courage, and gallant to a vanquished enemy. The heroine, in addition to physical beauty, possesses great ingenuity and bravery in high degree, and is devoted to her country, although this last trait is overshadowed by her desire to protect the man she loves.

The hero is engaged in espionage. He is shown as handsome, courageous, and gallant. In his relationship with the heroine, he makes a frank and honest effort to show her the pretense and sham with which she is surrounded. His outstanding characteristics are his courage and patriotism.

It will be noted that in three of these four cases the military crimes are presented in the highly glamorous rôle of espionage. Is it not fair to expect that some of this glamour will also be shed over the war in which they are engaged? If the reader does not believe that this hypothesis is a sound one, he is still faced with the fact that only one of these pictures shows the total results of such espionage. In this one picture the viewer gets a fleeting but vivid portrayal of how a single act of espionage causes the deaths of thousands of men. Knowing the power of the dramatic arts to mold men's minds, we may well pause and reflect seriously on the consequences which may accrue from this unrealistic portrayal of military crimes. On the other hand, we ought to express our appreciation for the portrayal of Sergeant Grischa in the motion picture by that name. There is presented here no glamour, no halo, only a gripping picture of the effect of the ravages of war upon a simple homesick peasant.

Eight leading characters who were criminals were rated as neither attractive nor unattractive. In other words, they fell between these two categories. Three of these were heroes, one was a heroine, two were other men, and two were villains. It is evident in this group then that the presentation here of criminal was neither white nor black. It was gray.

Twenty-one of the leading criminal characters are portrayed as unattractive. Interestingly enough, not one single member of this group is a hero or a heroine. The majority of them are villains or villainesses. Four are other men and women. Here are some descriptions of the unattractive characters:

The villain is a renegade who betrays a freight wagon train to the Indians. He is unattractive in appearance, a sullen, lowering person, treacherous and cruel.

One of the villain's victims, who had hired the villain to kill another man and had embezzled money from his firm, is a man of about forty, neatly enough dressed, but with a grim and scowling look about him. The story reveals that he is a man of harsh and bitter personality, rude to his wife and insolent to other people.

The villain in this picture, Injun Joe, is fearfully referred to by Tom Sawyer as "that murderin' half-breed." He is slovenly in appearance, shifty-eyed, with long stringy black hair, and is shown wearing a dilapidated pair of trousers and a nondescript shirt. In personality he is depicted as cruel, treacherous, and avaricious, as well as brooding, revengeful, and willing to commit any crime for money.

The villain, who had formerly maintained the heroine as his mistress, is a gangster. He is good-looking, extremely well-dressed, and lives in a luxurious apartment. His actions reveal him, however, as cruel and ruthless, committing one cold-blooded murder and attempting another, and finally, desperately trying to save himself at the expense of the heroine's happiness.

The villain, who is killed by the hero for the seduction of the hero's sister, is a sneering dandified figure. He is shown as cowardly, heartless, and lecherous.

The villain, who is the owner of the local saloon and the leader of a band of robbers, is suave and smooth-speaking. He dresses rather loudly, which contrasts with the cowboy clothing worn by the rest of the characters. His personal characteristics are shown as moral looseness and unscrupulousness, and he is depicted as a man who breaks his word, and will use any means to overcome his rival for the hand of the heroine.

The villain, whose nickname is "Handsome," is the good-looking, well-dressed leader of a gang of crooks operating on shipboard. He is pictured as sinister, revengeful, cynical, brooking no opposition to his plans.

What conclusions can now be drawn about the attractiveness of the leading male and female characters in the motion pictures? On the basis of the ratings checked (and it must be remembered that these were ratings by adults and *not by children*), 7 of the 37 criminals were portrayed as attractive. However, when we except from this group those involved in military crimes, only 3 remain. Further, 2 of the attractive heroes were placed in pictures which did not have a contemporary setting. One of the pictures was a Western; the other was laid in Russia during the Czarist régime. Therefore, only one picture remains in which the hero, a criminal, was definitely shown as attractive to adults.

All that can be said of the group of 8 leading characters that was classified as neither attractive nor unattractive is that they are criminals with both good and bad qualities. The effect of the picture itself upon an audience either of adults or of children is problematical. Twenty-one of the leading criminal characters, or almost two thirds of the total number, are classified by these adults as unattractive. Whether they would be so classified by children is open to question.

It is evident, however, that movie criminals are not always shown as low, cowardly, weak-minded, and physically repulsive. The evidence strongly suggests that no small proportion of the criminals are accomplished in some of the social graces, and many are well dressed. Not infrequently we see on the screen criminals who are courageous and who meet danger fearlessly.

The interpretation of these data is difficult. Common sense tells us that criminals are neither wholly good nor wholly bad. We cannot, therefore, expect the motion picture to show characters in a light other than that in which we know that they truly exist. Perhaps the major contribution of this phase of the study is the enlightenment of parents concerning the qualities of criminals. If they have trained their children properly to evaluate criminal behavior when seen on the screen, we need have no fear of undesirable outcomes. However, if they have failed to give this training, there is some reason to believe that the attractive qualities of a number of the leading characters may give children inaccurate data concerning crime and criminals.

What picture do the movies give us of the factors which cause criminality?

In almost every portrayal of criminals, they appear ready-made. Minerva-like they spring from the head of Jupiter, full-grown and often well-armed. Only rarely in the 40 pictures under discussion was there any indication that criminal patterns of behavior develop as a product of a long process of interaction between the individual and the successive social situations in which he lives. Since the pictures fail to portray this continuity of experience which produces the criminal, they cannot justifiably claim that they present an intelligent portrayal of the cause and cure of the crime problem.

The hard-boiled realism with which criminals are purportedly pictured in the films turns out to be a delusion. Instead, it is a pseudo-realism which mistakenly assumes that the standards of realism are adequately met by showing the blood spurting from a wound, the gun battles with the police, or the gallows on which the criminal is hanged. Data in the area where realism and objectivity are most needed— in setting forth adequate information on the causes and cures of crime—are sadly lacking. Almost never, for example, do crime pictures show unemployment and the attendant economic insecurity as a cause of crime. And yet a leading crime commission reports:

The conclusion seems inescapable that the assurance of economic security might be expected to bring with it an appreciable reduction in the volume of crime.[2]

Further, the causes of and cures for crime which do appear in motion pictures are often inadequate. Consider, for example, the following description of a scene from "Scarface," a highly touted gangster picture, a picture the mission of which was to present an "indictment of gang war in America":

A committee is conferring with a newspaper publisher. One of the men speaks up: "Our organizations are opposed to your policy, Mr. Garston. Your paper keeps right on playing up these killings as front-page news. You're glorifying the gangster by giving him all this publicity."

"That's ridiculous!" the publisher returns. "*You're* playing right into his hands. Show him up, run him right out of the country!"

"In the meantime," a woman puts in crisply, "you expect our children to read about gangsters and murder?"

"That's better than having them slaughtered!" Garston reminds her curtly.

There is then a discussion, which one man ends by protesting, "But what can our private citizens do? Even the police can't stop it."

"Don't blame the police!" the other exclaims. "They can't enforce laws that don't exist."

"Then it's up to the federal government," another man puts in.

Garston rises agitatedly. "*You* are the government. It's up to you to see that laws are passed that do some good. Put teeth in the deportation act. These gangsters don't belong in this country. Half of them aren't even citizens."

One man inquires in a disturbed tone what they can do, and the publisher exclaims, "All right, I'll tell you what to do. Make

[2] *Report on the Causes of Crime,* Vol. I, U. S. National Commission on Law Observance and Enforcement, Publication No. 13, p. 312.

laws and see that they are obeyed, if we have to have martial law to do it. The governor of New Mexico declared martial law to stop a bull fight; the governor of Oklahoma to regulate oil production. Surely gang war and wholesale law defiance are more of a menace to the nation than a bull fight. The Army will help, so will the American Legion. They offered their services two years ago, and nobody ever called on them. Let's get wise to ourselves—we're fighting organized murder!'"

This analysis of and remedy for the crime problem is absurdly naïve and perhaps socially dangerous. Summarized, it is as follows:

1. The newspaper and motion picture (implicitly) are showing up the gangster.
2. Children should read about gangsters and murder in order not to be slaughtered.
3. The police can do nothing since they can't enforce laws which do not exist.
4. Individuals ought to see to it that laws are passed which "will do some good." Make laws and see that they are obeyed.
5. The deportation of the gangsters who are not citizens will solve our crime problem.

The fundamental philosophy of movie criminology as presented in this highly popular gangster picture seems to be that the crimes are committed by bad people. Therefore, jail or deport all bad people and the crime problem is solved.

The writer has watched the screen carefully for pictures which attempt to give the viewer an insight into causes for crime. A few have given hints of causes. "I Am a Fugitive from a Chain Gang" shows unemployment as a cause. "Young America" gives a very sympathetic picture of the workings of a juvenile court.

We see in Table 35 the number of crimes per picture either committed or attempted. We note, for example, that 1 picture had 25 crimes and that 23 pictures had 1 crime. The total number of crimes either committed or attempted was 449.

TABLE 35

NUMBER OF CRIMES PER PICTURE EITHER COMMITTED OR ATTEMPTED IN THE 115 PICTURES

There was	1	crime in each of	23	pictures
There were	2	crimes in each of	21	pictures
There were	0	crimes in each of	18	pictures
There were	4	crimes in each of	13	pictures
There were	7	crimes in each of	10	pictures
There were	3	crimes in each of	8	pictures
There were	6	crimes in each of	6	pictures
There were	8	crimes in each of	3	pictures
There were	14	crimes in each of	3	pictures
There were	12	crimes in each of	2	pictures
There were	17	crimes in each of	2	pictures
There were	5	crimes in	1	picture
There were	9	crimes in	1	picture
There were	10	crimes in	1	picture
There were	13	crimes in	1	picture
There were	16	crimes in	1	picture
There were	25	crimes in	1	picture

There were 449 crimes in 115 pictures
84 per cent of the pictures (97 pictures) had 1 or more crime depicted

What specific crimes and violence are portrayed in motion pictures, and what techniques are presented for committing the crime and violence?

A common criticism of the movies is that violent methods are commonly used to settle disputes. The nature of the deaths by violence and the agents who commit such acts are shown in Table 36.

It should be pointed out that these include death by legal means, as well as illegal means. The table is read as follows:

The hero was responsible for causing 15 of the 71 deaths by violence. This is 21 per cent of the total number. He was responsible for 2 attempted deaths by violence, which is 7 per cent of a total number of 30. Further, he was responsible for 17, or 16.8 per cent, of the total committed or attempted deaths by violence.

Of the deaths by violence which were actually committed, the villain was responsible for 39 per cent; the villainess for

TABLE 36

DEATHS BY VIOLENCE IN THE 115 PICTURES

The number and per cent of crimes committed by each type of character

Character	Violent Deaths					
	Committed		Attempted		Total	
	Number	Per cent	Number	Per cent	Number	Per cent
Hero.........	15	21	2	7	17	16.8
Heroine......	1	1	2	7	3	3.0
Villain........	28	39	18	60	46	45.5
Villainess.....	4	6	1	3	5	5.0
Other men.....	16	23	5	17	21	20.8
A group......	7	10	2	7	9	8.9
Total.........	71	100	30	100	101	100

6 per cent; the heroine for 1 per cent; and other characters were responsible for 33 per cent. Deaths by violence occurred in 45 of the 115 pictures, or 39 per cent.

Techniques for the commission of crime are presented in many motion pictures. It will, therefore, be of interest to readers to survey the data in Table 37 which points out the techniques used to commit the murders in the 115 pictures which we analyzed.

A revolver was the most frequently used method of committing and attempting murder. A revolver was used for 20 murders in 18 different pictures, and was used in 9 pictures for 15 attempted murders. Committed and attempted murders with revolver appeared in 22 pictures for a total of

35 attempts. Further, the hero committed 9 of the revolver murders; the heroine, 1; the villain, 8; and other men, 2. Of the attempted murders, however, the hero committed only 1; the heroine, 2; the villain, 10; other men, 1; and a

TABLE 37

MURDER TECHNIQUES SHOWN IN THE 115 PICTURES

Distribution of techniques used in attempted and committed murders according to number of pictures, number of crimes, and type of characters

Technique	Committed									Attempted									Total	
	Agent							Number of Crimes	Number of Pictures	Agent							Number of Crimes	Number of Pictures	Number of Crimes	Number of Pictures
	Hero	Heroine	Villain	Villainess	Other Men	OtherWomen	A Group			Hero	Heroine	Villain	Villainess	Other Men	OtherWomen	A Group				
1 Revolver	9	1	8		2			20	18	1	2	10		1		1	15	9	35	22
2 Knifing			2	2	2			6	5			5		2			7	5	13	9
3 General shooting	1		3		2			6	5										6	5
4 Hanging				6				6	1				1				1	1	7	1
5 Stabbing			2			1		3	3										3	3
6 Beaten to death			2					2	2										2	2
7 Drowning	1				1			2	2										2	2
8 Fall			1					1	1			1					1	1	2	2
9 Indeterminate			1					1	1										1	1
10 Lynching	1							1	1			1					1	1	2	2
11 Machine gun												2					2	2	2	2
12 Strangling	1				1			2	2										2	2
13 Clubbing			1					1	1										1	1
14 Gored to death			1					1	1										1	1
15 Massacre							1	1	1										1	1
16 Pushed out of plane																1	1	1	1	1
17 Rifle			1					1	1										1	1
18 Run over by car												1					1	1	1	1
Total	13	1	22	8	8	1	1	54	35	1	2	20	1	3	0	2	29	17	83	44

group, 1. We can see reasons why 49 per cent of 110 criminals interviewed by Dr. Blumer said that the movies gave them the desire to carry a gun.[3]

Knifing was the second most popular method of murder

[3] Blumer, Herbert, and Hauser, Philip M., *Movies, Delinquency and Crime*, New York: The Macmillan Company, 1933 p. 71.

or attempted murder, occurring a total of 13 different times in 9 of the 115 pictures.

These figures, which deal only with murders, reveal strikingly that violent means are often used to settle disputes. Further, the hero and other characters are frequently shown as settling their problems in this fashion. Since Dr. Thurstone has shown that attitudes can be changed through the viewing of motion pictures,[4] it seems reasonable to believe that the continued display of murders may influence those who view such pictures. Not only is there a possibility that an attitude more favorable to crime may be thus developed, but there is also a possibility that life problems similar in nature to those seen in the movies will be settled by similar methods. In other words, the screen, in common with other methods of education, offers various suggestions for solving certain problems. It parades before our eyes a way of life. If the standards of the viewers are sufficiently well formed, there is a possibility that the changes which occur will be greatly minimized. When, however, immature persons see attractive characters solving life's problems through methods of violence, and if parents or others do not immediately supply antidotes, we may expect that the screen solution will have some influence on the action patterns of these individuals.

However, these techniques which are used for murder are probably far more significant from a point of view of mental hygiene than they are in terms of actual education in methods for committing murder. The possible harm that may be created is well illustrated in the returns from a questionnaire sent out under the direction of the Bureau of Child Research of the State University of Kansas, relating to the physical

---

[4] Peterson, Ruth C., and Thurstone, L. L., *Motion Pictures and the Social Attitudes of Children*, New York: The Macmillan Company, 1933.

effects of motion-picture attendance of children. The children had been asked to give reasons for their dislike of motion pictures. Samples of answers at the different age levels are as follows:

Nine-year-old boys: Killing—don't like to see people killed. Don't like to look at them.

Nine-year-old girls: Danger and killing. Look "offel." Not good for your mind. Scares me. I pity the people.

Ten-year-old boys: Killing—makes you too excited. Makes me sad. Wild west not good.

Ten-year-old girls: Killing—hate to see people killed. Don't like it. Makes me feel it's true. Scary. Bloody ones make me sick. Show you how to kill. Sad.

Eleven-year-old boys: Killing makes you have bad habits. Don't like blood. Like to laugh.

Eleven-year-old girls: Shooting and killing bad. Makes me scared to go anywhere after night. Makes me cry when I don't like to in front of so many people. Hard on the eyes and mind. Too tiresome. Too exciting. Hate to see people suffer. Not good for children.

Twelve-year-old boys: Killing reacts on the nervous system too much. Too sad.

Twelve-year-old girls: Shooting and killing makes me sick. It looks so awful to see people killed, and do not think it is right. Scares me. Not interested. Not good for children.

Thirteen-year-old boys: Too much killing—learn to do wrong things. Learn you to do stealing.[5]

When we turn now to a consideration of all the crimes committed in the motion pictures, including murder, we get the data presented in Table 38.

A glance at this table discloses a striking amount of crime

[5] Unpublished study, Bureau of Child Research, University of Kansas.

TABLE 38

TYPES OF CRIME COMMITTED OR ATTEMPTED IN THE 115 PICTURES

The number of each type of crime which was committed or attempted and the number of pictures in which each crime was shown

Type of Crime	Number of Crimes			Number of Pictures in Which Crimes Were		
	Committed	Attempted	Either Committed or Attempted	Committed	Attempted	Either Committed or Attempted
Murder..............	54	29	83	35	17	44
Assault and battery..	59		59	32		32
Gambling...........	36		36	17		17
Threatening with weapons	25		25	17		17
Kidnaping..........	21		21	14		14
Carrying concealed weapons..........	20		20	12		12
Holdup.............	17	1	18	12	1	12
Verbal threat to kill..	12		12	9		9
Suicide.............	9	2	11	7	2	9
Fighting with weapons	11		11	6		6
False pretenses......	11		11	7		7
Housebreaking.......	8		8	5		5
Embezzlement.......	8		8	6		6
Swindling..........	6	2	8	4	1	5
Accomplice to crime..	5	2	7	5	1	5
Treason............	7		7	6		6
General robbery.....	6		6	2		2
Blackmail..........	5	1	6	4	1	5
Prison or jailbreak...	6		6	4		4
Racketeering.......	5		5	5		5
Espionage..........	5		5	3		3
Seduction...........	2	2	4	2	2	4
Safe-breaking.......	3	1	4	1	1	2
Jewel robbery.......	4		4	2		2
Cattle rustling......	4		4	3		3
Bribery............	3	1	4	2	1	3
Grave-robbing.......	3		3	1		1
Petty thievery......	3		3	2		2
Forgery............	3		3	3		3
Destruction of property..............	3		3	3		3
Rebellion (military crime)............	3		3	1		1
Torture.............	2		2	2		2
Third degree........	2		2	2		2

TABLE 38—*Continued*

TYPES OF CRIME COMMITTED OR ATTEMPTED IN THE 115 PICTURES

Type of Crime	Number of Crimes			Number of Pictures in Which Crimes Were		
	Committed	Attempted	Either Committed or Attempted	Committed	Attempted	Either Committed or Attempted
Highway robbery....	2		2	1		1
Bank robbery.......	1	1	2	1	1	2
Auto stealing........	2		2	2		2
Horse stealing.......	2		2	1		1
Naval offenses.......	2		2	1		1
Mutiny.............	2		2	1		1
Burglary...........	2		2	2		2
Counterfeiting.......	2		2	1		1
Frame-up..........	2		2	1		1
Rum-running........	2		2	1		1
Drugs.............	2		2	2		2
Absent without leave	2		2	2		2
Traffic violations....	2		2	2		2
Receiving stolen goods	1		1	1		1
Breaking contract....	1		1	1		1
Bootlegging........	1		1	1		1
Hi-jacking.........		1	1		1	1
Overstepping caste bounds..........	1		1	1		1
Disturbing peace....	1		1	1		1
Perjury.............	1		1	1		1
Cruelty to children..	1		1	1		1
Desertion from army.	1		1	1		1
Offenses against mails	1		1	1		1
Solicitation........	1		1	1		1
Total...............	406	43	449	95	24	97

and violence. Murder, the most extreme form of violence, is at the top, in number of crimes committed as well as in number of crimes attempted. Assault and battery is second, and is committed in 32 pictures. Forty-three crimes are attempted and 406 committed, truly a large number. Further, we note that 97 of the 115 pictures or 84 per cent contain some form of crime or violence. No comments will be made on the remaining data, but study will reveal that motion pictures present to their viewers almost every conceivable type of crime.

These are the facts. What inferences can be drawn from the data?

The producers of these pictures and their spokesmen might well make this defense: Crime is indeed a social fact. Crime is excessive in real life. Therefore, if we are to depict real life on the screen, why not include crime in its actual magnitude? Further, we are not the only ones who are putting a great deal of emphasis on crime. Any large metropolitan daily will contain an account of at least one murder. Indeed, one could go through this same daily and find there an account of almost every crime that is contained here on this list.

A further defense made by these groups would be the statement that consequences of the commission of crime are shown in these pictures, thereby ensuring the desired moral effect. Certain weaknesses of this argument are shown by the writer on page 144.

Those who object to this emphasis on crime and violence on the screen would perhaps state their arguments as follows: There is no objection to showing crime as a social fact, but there is grave danger that due to this excessive and dramatic way of presenting crime, those whose judgments are immature and unformed may be given an acquaintanceship with crime that tends to give them a very incorrect notion about modern life. They are likely to conclude that all life is inconsiderate, intolerant, and brutish. Such a view is likely to breed a lack of confidence in one's fellow men, to develop unwholesome suspicions, to interfere with a normal emotional development, to foster distrust.

Persons who are so influenced will fail to see society as fundamentally wholesome, happy, promising. They will not catch a vision of a cheerful, coöperative society, built by persons who are able to face reality. It is likely to breed an apathetic pessimism, instead of a buoyant optimism. It may develop a mental set of defeatism, thus discouraging improvement.

Children's play patterns may be affected by viewing motion pictures in which violence plays a prominent part. Instead of imaginative, sensitive, creative play, we shall have violent play, wholly devoid of imagination, coarse and imitative in nature. Instead of developing a type of play in which individuals get some pattern of an ideal which holds that human effort counts, which advances the theory that one individual, even single-handed, can do a great deal in this world, rather it develops the pattern in which shooting, catching, or punishing the criminal will play a large part.

That crime in motion pictures can be definitely labeled excessive is suggested by the effect which it has upon the person who has not yet formed satisfactory judgments about American life. We have but to turn to accounts of foreigners upon coming to this country, or previous to their coming, to see how they have been influenced unfavorably and inaccurately by our movies. One Japanese visitor during the Olympic Games reported to me that a number of his countrymen visiting one of our large cities, were at first loath to leave the hotel in the evenings because of their fear of the gangsters they had seen in American movies.

We must ask, therefore, about these 449 attempted and committed crimes: Do they tend to develop in individuals strong insight into our crime problem and methods of solving it? Do they actually refresh and invigorate the viewers, or do they tend to give untutored minds the opinion that we live in a diseased and disordered society, a condition from which there is no retreat?

What crime techniques are shown in motion pictures?

A common criticism of motion pictures is that they present detailed crime techniques to the viewers, and that motion pictures are a school for crime. What does our analysis of crime pictures show, relative to crime techniques?

The answer to this question is somewhat difficult, since one hardly knows how to define the term "technique." That there is a high incidence of crime and methods for commission of crime in motion pictures is illustrated, first of all, by pointing out that there are 406 crimes committed and 43 additional ones attempted in 97 of the 115 pictures which we studied. Further, a glance at Table 38 will show that 54 murders were committed in 35 of the pictures, and 29 others attempted in 17 pictures.

There is perhaps little value in recounting, detail by detail, the specific crime techniques utilized under each of these reported criminal activities. Two or three groups will be selected, however, and the methods detailed.

The first group of techniques relates to robbery and swindling. There were, for example, 8 people who participated in housebreaking in 5 pictures. The methods used in the 5 cases were as follows: In 3 cases there was unlawful entry without breaking in. In one case the hero entered the heroine's hotel room through a window. In the fifth case the hero broke the window glass and entered a public building.

Techniques for robbery, other than those thus far mentioned, are as follows:

> A gang of robbers hold up a restaurant, gag the employees, and take all the money that they find.
> The Kinkajou gang robs a bank at Fremont.
> The cattle are rustled and their tracks obliterated by swimming the animals through a stream.

A young man plans with friends to have them rob him of bonds which he is carrying.

Two men masquerade as stage-hands in a theater, and switch off the lights for the robbery which is committed by a confederate.

A plane equipped with machine guns forces down another plane, and takes the spark plugs from the plane in order to avoid pursuit.

Stolen securities are smuggled ashore by planting one of the gang among the engine-room crew and letting him take them ashore when the boat docks.

A young man borrows his employer's limousine and chauffeur without the owner's permission, in order to create an impression upon the heroine.

A bandit props up a rifle in order to convey the impression that a second man is assisting him in holding up a stagecoach.

There were 6 instances of swindling involving 8 people. The techniques were as follows:

Fake medical cures to stimulate trade.

The hero poses as a woman's long-lost son in order to swindle her out of her money.

A fake bill of sale is used to sell cattle.

A banker absconds to Europe with securities when his banking firm fails.

The villain sells fake statuary to the hero's son.

The villain uses his power of attorney to purchase land from a client at a low price, and he in turn sells it to a real estate firm at a large profit.

The techniques used to commit the 9 suicides found in 115 pictures are as follows: Two end their lives by the use of a revolver, 2 by stabbing, 1 by jumping out of a window, 1 by gas, 1 by poison, 1 by suicidal disobedience of a doctor's orders, and 1 by deliberate exposure to the elements.

Do these data indicate that the motion pictures are a

school for crime? The answer is difficult. Certainly it is true that the motion pictures suggest a variety of different areas in which crimes are committed. However, the methods for commission vary greatly in detail. Some do give highly specialized technical information, such as°smuggling a note to a man in jail in a package of cigarettes, hiding opium in a flower pot, enticing a victim to a hotel room by means of a fake telephone call, rubbing the door knob to obliterate finger prints, escaping from jail by creating confusion among the men, sliding the key of a locked door on a string back into the room in order to convey the impression that an injured man inside the room has locked himself in.

These examples are given to demonstrate clearly that some specialized methods of committing crimes are presented in motion pictures. However, the point can easily be labored. One could hardly maintain with much force that the amount of crime committed in this country was directly a function of knowledge or lack of knowledge of specialized methods. Certainly, however, we might expect that the visualization of exact methods of commission, by their smoothness, may induce some persons to try them. Detailed evidence of this type of influence is presented by Dr. Blumer in his report. No matter what the effect may be on the viewer of detailed methods of crime commission, we do have ample evidence in this analysis of 115 pictures that tremendous amounts of crime of varied sorts are committed therein.

PUNISHMENT FOR MAJOR CRIMES

Table 39 indicates the punishments received by the leading characters in the 40 pictures analyzed in detail. It will be noted that out of a total of 62 characters who commit crimes, 15 received no punishment at all. Eighteen are arrested but 8 of them are either released or escape. The punishment of

7 is inferred. It will be noted that in the case of only 5 of the 62 was the legal punishment carried out.

The reader will be interested in getting more detail on the nature of the crimes and their punishment. These are

TABLE 39

PUNISHMENT OF CRIMINALS IN THE 40 PICTURES

The number and per cent of criminals who received each type of punishment

Type of Punishment	Number	Per cent
No punishment............................	15	24.2
Arrested—Held............................	3	4.9
Arrested—Released........................	4	6.4
Arrested—Escaped........................	4	6.4
Arrested—Punishment inferred..............	7	11.3
Legal punishment carried out...............	5	8.1
Extra-legal punishment		
As a direct result of the crime............	6	9.7
More or less accidental..................	17	27.4
Personal revenge......................	1	1.6
Total...........................	62	100

discussed under military crimes, murders, attempted murders, kidnaping, robbery, embezzlement, housebreaking, blackmail, and miscellaneous.

MILITARY CRIMES

Out of the 40 pictures, there were 5 which contained crimes associated with military situations. Of these, 2 involved espionage, carried on by both the heroes and one of the heroines. In both of the pictures the hero was arrested and sentenced to face a firing squad, but in one he was rescued by the timely arrival of his troops, and in the other the heroine assisted him in escaping. The heroine engaged in espionage was also captured by the enemy and sentenced to die before a firing squad, but managed to drug the hero and make her escape.

Three pictures dealt with treason. In one, the hero is arrested and convicted of treason, sentenced to face a firing squad, but escapes by a clever ruse. In another picture, the villain is guilty of treason, but is not captured, and dies an accidental death. In the third picture, the heroine is arrested, convicted, and shot by a firing squad.

The hero of another picture escapes from a prison camp, is captured, and dies at the hands of a firing squad. Still another hero is arrested for being absent without leave, but no further punishment is shown and he is later released.

Thus we see that of the 3 people engaged in espionage, all were captured and sentenced to death, but either escaped or were rescued. Of the 3 convicted of treason, the heroine was executed by a firing squad, the hero was sentenced to death but escaped, and the villain was accidentally killed. One hero was shot for escaping from a prison camp, and another hero was arrested for being absent without leave, but suffered no further punishment.

MURDERS

Out of the 40 pictures, there are 13 which include a murder, and 9 in which there are murder attempts. The latter pictures include some of the former, although when the same character both attempts a murder and commits one, he is tabulated as being punished only for the actual commission of the crime.

In these pictures, only 3 heroes commit murders. One hero escapes punishment entirely; another is given a life sentence to the penitentiary, and the third is shot in a gun battle with the villain, both dying simultaneously.

None of the heroines in the 40 pictures commit a murder,

but 8 villains are involved in such a situation. Their fates are as follows: Villain No. 1 is arrested at the end of the picture, and the inference is that he will be fittingly punished, although the punishment is not shown. Villain No. 2 is shot in a gun battle with the hero, whom he also kills. Villain No. 3 is arrested, convicted, and given a life sentence to the penitentiary, but he later escapes, only to be killed in a gun battle with detectives. Villain No. 4 is not apprehended, as he has made the murder seem a suicide. Villain No. 5 is arrested, and the inference is that he will be punished. Villain No. 6 is also arrested for murder, and it is inferred that he will be punished. Villain No. 7 escapes during the trial, when evidence which involves him comes to light, and later meets his death by an accidental fall over a cliff.

Another murder is committed by a woman, who is arrested at the end of the picture, and again the inference is that she will be punished. A villainess commits a murder, and at the end of the picture is accidentally killed. Two other murders are committed by men characters, 1 of whom is not punished, although he later commits suicide for another reason, while the other is arrested and is awaiting trial during the picture.

The remaining murders fall in a "group" classification. One was committed by a group of Russian outlaws, and the other was an Indian massacre in which a number of people were killed.

ATTEMPTED MURDERS

We felt it desirable to include murder attempts, as well as the actual murders, but it must be kept in mind that the punishments listed generally follow crimes other than the attempted killing.

No murder attempts were made by a hero, and only 1 by a

heroine, a spy who attempts to shoot the hero, an enemy spy. She is later executed for treason.

Here again the majority of such situations involve the villain, 6 such characters having attempted murder. Their punishments follow: Villain No. 1 is shot in a gun battle with the hero, whom he had attempted to lynch; Villain No. 2 is arrested and awaiting punishment for robbery; Villain No. 3 is arrested at the end of the picture as a gangster, punishment inferred; Villain No. 4 is killed during a skirmish with natives in Morocco; Villain No. 5 is killed in a gun battle resulting from the robbery of the air express; Villain No. 6 is wounded in a gun battle with the hero, but his final punishment is indeterminate.

KIDNAPING

Another major crime fairly common in these pictures is kidnaping. This crime is committed by 2 of the heroes, 1 of whom is captured and flogged, but later released; while the other is not punished. Four villains are involved in similar situations, with the following results: Villain No. 1 is shot in a gun battle with the hero; Villain No. 2 is arrested as a gangster and his punishment inferred; Villain No. 3 is not punished; Villain No. 4 is killed in a gun battle resulting from the robbery of the air express. No kidnapings are carried on by other characters. All the persons kidnaped are adults.

ROBBERY

Under this heading are grouped various types of robbery, including highway robbery, auto stealing, cattle rustling, jewel robbery, and so forth. Four heroes are involved in crimes of this nature, two receiving no punishment while another is shot in a gun battle with the villain; and the third is given a two-year sentence to the penitentiary.

Three villains also engage in robbery. Villains No. 1 and 2 are killed in gun battles, and Villain No. 3 is wounded in a gun battle with the hero, but it was impossible to determine what further punishment was meted out.

Two men characters are involved in robberies, and both are shot in gun battles.

The remaining crimes in this division might be called "group" robberies. The first group is not apprehended; it was not possible to determine what punishment the second group received; while in the third group, one man is arrested, but the punishment of the others, though vaguely inferred, also could not be definitely determined.

EMBEZZLEMENT

Another prevalent crime is embezzlement. One hero is involved, but he is not prosecuted as he decides to personally make restitution. A heroine is guilty of this crime, but repents at the end of the picture and suffers no punishment. A villain is also involved in embezzlement, and neither repents nor is punished. The remaining 3 occurrences involve other men characters, one of whom suffers no punishment; one is shot by the villain for other reasons; and the third is also murdered by the villain.

HOUSEBREAKING

Of 2 other heroes who are involved in a similar situation, 1 suffers no punishment, while the other is arrested and held on suspicion.

BLACKMAIL

A villainess commits blackmail, along with a number of other crimes, and is accidentally killed. A man who attempts it in another picture is murdered by the villain, whom he is seeking to defraud.

MISCELLANEOUS

Inasmuch as each of the following crimes occurs only once, they are dealt with in a group. A man commits forgery; a hero leads a mutiny; another man commits bribery. All go unpunished. A villain commits a seduction, and is killed by the wronged girl's brother. Another villain turns renegade, betrays a wagon train to the Indians, and is killed in the battle which ensues. Still another villain swindles various persons, and is in turn swindled by the hero, under threat of arrest if he protests. A man is shown bootlegging, and is arrested at the end of the picture. A hero and heroine purchase liquor on Rum Row, attempt to run it through, are apprehended by Federal authorities, but are later released although no reason is indicated in the picture.

CONCLUSION

These data show very clearly that the criminal is not always punished in the motion pictures, and any claim that he is flies in the face of facts. However, the writer does not believe that this necessarily constitutes a criticism of motion pictures. If the motion-picture drama is to have the right to depict crime as a "social fact," it must have the right to tell the truth. And there is little doubt that the criminal is apprehended just as frequently in the motion picture as he is in real life, and perhaps even more frequently.

There may be some danger, of course, in permitting immature children to see the criminal "getting away with it." Yet they need only be able to read to see that he does get away with it in real life. However, instead of placing emphasis on realism in regard to a lack of punishment, the motion-picture screen might well depict the consequences other than those involving punishment that flow from crime. This they fail to do.

Shall we then entirely eliminate crime from the screen? Such a view is as unintelligent as one which would maintain that by overemphasizing crime on the screen we shall thus bring the American public to a realization of the tremendous amount of crime which is committed in this country.

It appears to the writer that one of the major values of the portrayal of crime is to clarify its undesirable consequences not merely to the criminal but to all of society and to inspire the audience with an ambition to develop a society more immune to its ravages. Such a motion-picture drama might develop zest, energy, and enthusiasm for the improvement of our social order. It might picture the better promise of the society in which we may some time live. It would portray the causes and cures for crime realistically but with appropriate emphasis.

Some readers will object to this point of view and insist that it is not the function of the screen to educate the public in regard to crime. Instead, they will say that violent emotion expressed on the screen represents a catharsis, a purging of the emotions, an escape from life, that it has no meaning at all in terms of general improvement of society. They will maintain that one approaches a murder mystery or a crime story in much the same way that he would seek enjoyment out of assembling a jig-saw puzzle.

The escape motif of current recreational life will not be discussed at length. Suffice it to say that the conception of movies as a national aspirin indicates a very low conception of the function of recreation in an industrial civilization. This attempt to fit people to live in our current world by temporarily paralyzing their mental and emotional natures at a time when, as never before, we need to make minds clearer, is an abdication of the responsibility of every citizen. This temporary paralysis, this temporary flight from reality, this running away from the world, not only merely postpones the solution of the problem but actually may unfit that individual to take his place as a responsible member of society. A strong case, therefore, can be made for the present type of crime pictures as a dangerous kind of opium.

Such a point of view is not contrary to the utilization of motion pictures to give renewed freshness and vigor to life. Through the arts one may secure a refreshed readiness for a more vigorous attack on serious problems. But such excursions into the field of art are wholesome in so far as they make possible later continuous, serious effort in thinking about problems which face all of us. The power of any nation lies in its ability vigorously and straightforwardly to attack the critical problems of life. If motion pictures thwart or devitalize this power, they deserve only our strongest condemnation.

SUMMARY

The facts about crime in the movies are gathered from the study of the 1,500 pictures released during the years 1920, 1925, and 1930; from the 115 pictures which were actually viewed and from the 40 of these which were selected for detailed study.

The number of crime pictures has increased slightly since 1920. In 1930 approximately one fourth of the pictures dealt with crime as their major theme. The majority of criminals portrayed were judged to be unattractive by adults who read descriptions of these characters.

In 97 of the 115 pictures, 449 crimes were attempted or committed. The largest number of crimes in one picture was 25. The villain was responsible for almost one half of the violent deaths which were attempted or committed. The majority of such deaths were at the hands of the male characters. Eighteen techniques for committing murder were shown. The revolver was by far the most common. Fifty-seven types of crimes were shown. *Murder* was the first in rank; *assault and battery*, the second. Interestingly enough, in spite of the emphasis on sex pictures, *solicitation* was shown in only one instance.

In the 40 pictures almost one fourth of the criminals received no punishment and in over one fourth the punishment was more or less accidental.

The picture of crime given in the movies is of immense significance. We have seen in studies of the influence of movies on conduct that many young criminals learned their techniques from the motion picture. Others stated that they determined to become criminals because the movie criminal usually got off without punishment. From the data here presented we see that although it is not true that the movie criminal usually escapes punishment, the figures plainly show that a significant proportion do.

On the other hand any medium which attempts to portray life cannot avoid taking crime into consideration. A truthful and accurate account which showed causes and consequences in a large social sense might aid in the solution of the crime problem.

Certainly, in view of the large proportion of crime pictures and the findings of other studies, parental guidance of the movie attendance of children and youth is imperative.

CHAPTER IX

VULGARITY IN THE MOVIES

ANY study of vulgarity is hazardous. What is vulgarity? The Webster Dictionary defines it as "the state or quality of being coarse or common." The American Oxford Dictionary defines "vulgar" as "offending against refinement or good taste." We see at once that the problem of varying standards among different groups stares us in the face. Further, we must also face the dilemma of double meanings. Who shall determine whether any vulgarity was intended? The proverb says, "To the evil, all things are evil."

We have attempted to meet this dilemma in two ways. First of all we are using as one of our standards of inclusion of *possible* vulgarity those activities which a group of selected individuals characterize as such. Therefore, no inclusions of vulgarity are here made which are not so considered by at least three such individuals. Further, most of these inclusions were snickered or laughed at when they were flashed on the screen. The double meaning, therefore, does not exist only in the minds of the individuals who selected them.

Some of these statements of vulgarity will seem exceedingly tame to some of our readers. No charge of harmfulness is made by the writer. He does not say that any or all of them should be omitted from the pictures. For some of them the exclusion or inclusion is primarily one of convention. It may be considered vulgar today and inoffensive tomorrow. Others will greatly shock some individuals. This does not prove that they should be excluded. In other words,

154

the writer does not set down here his personal standards for exclusion and inclusion, because his standards may reflect only a minority opinion. He does, however, present the evidence and prefers to let the readers decide what they consider good and bad taste.

He does wish to present the following hypotheses concerning these materials. First of all, the charge that certain of these vulgarities, especially the double meanings, are above the heads of children must be carefully considered. It is sometimes true that they are. However, the fact that merriment or embarrassed laughter follows certain of the sallies provokes learning. Thus the child becomes sensitized to certain remarks because he has been conditioned by previous experiences. This fact cannot be disregarded when one is trying to evaluate the effect of these vulgarities. Children will learn to laugh at the things their elders laugh at. Some will say, why not? Others believe that the effects are undesirable.

That obscenity and vulgarity are exceedingly difficult to define is very clearly indicated in the various court decisions relating to books and pictures that are supposedly vulgar or obscene. Further, one need only note the great shifts permitted in language and scenes in the theater to realize the changes that occur over a period of time. In view of the fact that the current mores vary so greatly in reference to this problem we shall omit an extended treatment of this topic. We shall, however, present the classifications of three adults for what they may be worth. Table 40 indicates the categories into which the "vulgar" incidents are distributed, and the number of pictures in which such incidents were found. It is read as follows: Thirteen pictures, or 33 per cent, contain 14 hinted improper sex relationships, comprising 20 per cent of all vulgar incidents. It will be noted further that there is a total of 70 vulgar incidents in the 40 pictures, and that they are distributed among 13 areas. One or more vulgarity is found in 65 per cent of the pictures.

In order that the reader may gain some notion of the type of item classified under each of these categories, two samples

TABLE 40

VULGARITY IN THE 40 PICTURES

The number and per cent of pictures and of incidents in which each type of vulgarity was seen

	Incidents		Pictures	
	Number	Per cent	Number	Per cent
Hinted improper sex relationships	14	20	13	33
Sex reference to man's or woman's body	12	17	10	25
References to anatomy	11	16	5	13
References to bridal night	6	9	4	10
Bathroom humor	5	7	4	10
References to babies	5	7	2	5
References to "dirty" stories	3	4	3	8
Reference to clothing	3	4	3	8
Sex potency	3	4	2	5
References to legitimacy of birth	2	3	2	5
Crudities	2	3	2	5
Nose thumbing	2	3	2	5
Sophisticated reaction to sex irregularity	2	3	1	3
Total	70	100	26	65

are given for each type. The incidents have been selected with a view to giving the best illustration of the type of "vulgarity" shown in the picture. It is clear, of course, that presenting these incidents in cold type fails to give the reader a satisfactory impression of the net effect of the film which has the advantage not only of the spoken word but also of intonation and gestures.

Hinted Improper Sex Relationships

As the door closes, Sigrid turns on Monty in a white fury, but he merely says apologetically, "Sigrid—did I do wrong?" She shrieks that she is ruined, and he protests affectionately, "Darling, you're not blaming *me* for that?"

"Headache?" he inquires solicitously.

"Oh, yes, and it's all your fault," she exclaims; then, as he starts to massage her head, "No, no, no! Don't do that. Don't do that! No, no, no, no, no, no! No—oh, oh—oh—ohhhh!" She makes little moans of contentment as he starts to massage her face. "That feels good. Oh, oh, that feels even better. Oh——oh, you must have electricity in your hands. Ohhh, I never felt like this before—gorgeous!"

The maid is listening outside the door, with a shocked and puzzled expression on her face.

Sex References to Man's or Woman's Body

He returns the watch to its owner, and a girl in the audience inquires of her neighbor in a whisper, "Do you suppose he can see through that black bandage?"

"If he can," she replies briefly, "this is no place for a lady with a thin skirt."

"You haven't changed," he declares, letting his eyes rove over her. "You still have the same inimitable lines."

"Yes, and you are still fond of reading between the lines," she jeers.

References to Anatomy

At this moment one of the usherettes sneezes and drops her handkerchief. As she starts to bend over to retrieve it, the theater manager yells, "Halt! With your figure and our pants, you should bend from the knees—so!" He illustrates his order, and the girl bends as he suggests and picks up her handkerchief.

In a minute, Axel Bronstrup again approaches Professor Willow and Barbara and says that since he was injured in football practice this afternoon Mr. Bentley will substitute for him on this dance. Barbara's face darkens, and she turns to Axel and suggests, "Perhaps Mr. Bronstrup would like to sit the dance out."

"Sure," Axel agrees quickly, but Biff Bentley kicks him viciously on the leg, and he hurriedly concludes, "only that is where I was injured!"

References to Bridal Night

"And you," turning to Mr. Forbes, "may have the bridal suite."

"What for?" grunts Mr. Forbes, and Dulcy shakes her finger at him in playful reproach.

"Now stop botherin' 'em," Seth admonishes the crowd. "How would you like to be a bride and be bothered all night?" There is a roar of laughter at this sally.

Bathroom Humor

Van Dyke's luggage is turned over to the butler and Dulcy asks him if he wouldn't like to go to his room and wash up. He says, "I won't wash, but I will go upstairs."

A moment after they join Rondelle at the plane, Frisky starts back toward the dugout, calling out that he forgot something.

"Say Frisky—take one for me," Hanson calls facetiously.

References to Babies

Trixie then asks if she had told Bob about "the big event," and when Marcia says no, orders, "Well, run on home and tell him because if I was a man and was going to have a baby, I'd want to know about it. Now beat it, Mrs. Henderson."

"Well, but some day I'm going to have a wife and kids," he declares solemnly.

"Well, even so, twelve rooms will be too many."

"I don't think so," Olsen stammers, twisting his hat, and the lawyer laughs helplessly.

References to "Dirty" Stories

The boys greet them relievedly and as they start up the stairs together, the brunette remarks, "Say, let's get going—I want to see this town of yours. I've been hearing some of those traveling men stories."

The two men, both smoking, stroll along together, Frisky chuckling, "Say, if it's the one about the dame who said her husband wasn't home, I've heard it."

References to Clothing

She tells him that the other girls in the show will razz her. "I guess you've never dressed in a room with twenty girls!" she cries, and Biff looks at her in astonishment.

At this, the fat detective starts going through his pockets, exclaiming, "Where is it? Where is it?" He finally pulls out the bit of ribbon, remarking relievedly, "Here, it's a good thing you asked me for it. If my old lady found that on me, say listen—"

The girl takes the ribbon and pulls up her dress, requesting, "Hold that, will you—"

"I will not," he replies indignantly, as she starts to thread the ribbon in the bottom of her panties.

Sex Potency

Three conductors are standing in the train passage, laughing and talking. The man who knocked at the Countess' compartment holds up his hand and exclaims, "Listen—here's a puzzle, and believe me it's hot. She comes from a wedding—she has nothing on—she's left her husband behind—she has no ticket— she has no idea where she wants to go, and she goes to Monte Carlo. How old is her husband?" He pauses a moment and the other two regard him expectantly. "Too old!" he declares, and all three of them go into spasms of laughter.

Legitimacy of Birth

Morehouse disgustedly puts his glasses back on, then uneasily asks the butler what the word "pater" means. When the servant informs him that it means "father," he says relievedly, "Oh, I thought it was some newfangled way of questioning the legitimacy of my birth."

Crudities

As the two old scouts approach, they offer them a drink, Jim declaring, "The man what don't drink with us is a double-bladdered skunk."

A mechanic informs Pierce that the dirigible has signaled for the plane to hook itself on. He throws his cigarette away and turns toward the plane, remarking to Rondelle, "Pardon me while I imitate a baby pig hooking onto its mama pig for lunch."

Nose Thumbing

The boy thanks him politely and, as soon as his back is turned, deliberately thumbs his nose at the player who had criticized him.

Frisky derisively thumbs his nose at Bradon, who continues his bantering.

Sophisticated Reaction to Sex Irregularity

While they are checking their wraps, one of the girls exclaims derisively, "So this is one of the places where women wallow in sin!"

In Billy's office the girls are sitting on the desk, discussing whether or not Lem spent the night at a hotel. Tom asks why he would go there, and one of the girls asks brightly, "Why do they have hotels?" She then proposes a debate on this subject, and Tom half-laughingly tries to choke her.

The motion-picture industry would probably reply to these statements of vulgarity much in the way of the following editorial from the *Film Daily* of August 23, 1932:[1]

It is rather amusing, this nonsensical tornado of horse-feathers about filth in pictures. One can pause but a second to realize how little smut, comparatively, there is on the present-day screen. Compared to the literature of the hour, the commercial advertisements of the times, the artistic conception of the day and the legitimate stage, the average talking picture has

[1] Jack Alicoate, "Smut . . . and other things," *Film Daily*, August 23, 1932.

been rinsed to the point of milky white cleanliness. As times change, so do thoughts and morals. The conventional doings of 1932 would be scandals of a few years back. For this industry to miss the pulse of the hour would be fatal. We have, in this column, waged a constant fight against vulgarity and dirt in production, but we do feel that this industry is paying entirely too much attention to those long haired reformers who would dress our screen in corsets and flannel petticoats. The world moves with the pulse of the times. So must the screen.

SUMMARY

The study of vulgarity was confined to the 40 pictures which were studied intensively. The procedure was to have three adults select those incidents which they considered vulgar. Only those incidents which were independently selected by all three observers were used. In 65 per cent of the pictures one or more vulgar incident occurred. Thirteen types of vulgarity were noted, the most frequent being *hinted improper sex relationships*.

Because of the changing of standards from time to time and from place to place, it is difficult to speak with finality about vulgarity. The reader may judge for himself whether or not he feels that the incidents so classified are vulgar. If he does not, the figures here presented will be too high. However, there may have been instances which were not tabulated as being vulgar which would be offensive to some persons. For these persons the figures would be low.

If the figures are accepted, the next question is whether or not the occurrence of vulgar incidents in about two out of three pictures is too high. Compared to that found in other forms of amusement, the movie percentage of vulgarity may be low. However, the writer is inclined to believe that anything which is truly offensive to good taste is better not included.

CHAPTER X

RECREATIONS, LIQUOR AND TOBACCO IN THE MOVIES

RECREATIONS IN THE MOVIES

WHAT are the chief recreations of the leading men and women characters in the 40 pictures analyzed in detail? Such activities may have some effect upon the recreations of those who view these recreational activities on the screen. The recreational activities have been divided into three groups: indoor, outdoor, and miscellaneous. The data are presented in Tables 41, 42, and 43.

TABLE 41

INDOOR RECREATIONS OF THE LEADING CHARACTERS IN THE 40 PICTURES

Number of each type of character indulging in each type of recreation and the number and per cent of the pictures in which each type of recreation was shown

| Type of Recreation | Number of Characters | | | | | | | | Pictures | |
	Hero	Heroine	Villain	Villainess	Other Men	Other Women	Group	Total	Number	Per cent
Dancing.....	11	12	1	1	12	10	11	58	16	40.0
Having tea...	6	5			2	1	3	17	9	22.5
Drawing.....		1						1	1	2.5
Painting.....		1						1	1	2.5
Attending Theater ...	1	4	2		4	1	1	13	4	10.0
Opera.....	2	2	1				1	6	2	5.0

162

TABLE 41—*Continued*

INDOOR RECREATIONS OF THE LEADING CHARACTERS IN THE 40 PICTURES

Type of Recreation	Number of Characters								Pictures	
	Hero	Heroine	Villain	Villainess	Other Men	Other Women	Group	Total	Number	Per cent
Attending Church....	1		1			1	2	5	1	2.5
Flower show....		1			1			2	1	2.5
Movies....	1	1					1	3	1	2.5
Prize-fight.	1	1			1		1	4	1	2.5
Playing Piano.....	2	7		1	5	1		16	11	27.5
Banjo.....					3			3	3	7.5
Guitar.....	1							1	1	2.5
Harmonica				1				1	1	2.5
Violin.....		1						1	1	2.5
Playing Poker.....			1		3		3	7	3	7.5
Solitaire...					3			3	3	7.5
Billiards...	2			1	2			5	2	5.0
Roulette...	3	2	1				3	0	2	5.0
Analogies..	1	1					1	3	1	2.5
Bridge.....	1	1			2			4	1	2.5
Dominoes..					2			2	1	2.5
Games....	1	1			1	1	1	5	1	2.5
Listening to Radio.....	1	4	1	1	1	1	1	9	8	20.0
Singer.....	1	1	1	1	1		1	6	2	5.0
Reading Book......	1	1			1			3	3	7.5
Newspaper	1		2					3	3	7.5
Magazine..		1						1	1	2.5
Total........	38	48	10	6	44	16	30	192	34	85.0

It will be noted in the indoor recreations group that dancing is found in 40 per cent of the 40 pictures, playing the piano in 27.5 per cent, having tea in 22.5 per cent, and listening to the radio in 20 per cent.

Dancing is probably high not only because it is exemplified as a leisure-time activity of the well-to-do, but also because it provides a welcome relief from dialogue by constantly shifting the scene of action. Further, it involves the introduction of music, an additional feature of interest. The reason for the presence of piano playing to the exclusion of other musical instruments, with the exception of the radio, perhaps is due to the fact that the piano is one of the few musical instruments which require no accompaniment. Further, it may be an accomplishment with which a good many of the stars are endowed. Perhaps the best reason is that it offers a plausible method for introducing a pleasing break in the monotony of straight dialogue.

It is interesting to note that four motion pictures showed leading characters attending the theater and only one showed them attending the movies. Is one to infer that the motion-picture producers themselves think that the public believes that it is much smarter to attend the theater than to attend the movies?

Reading newspapers, books, and magazines does not rank high as an activity. Is this because there is little motion involved? Is it because the director thinks it not wise to identify his characters as people who read books?

In Table 42 are represented the outdoor sports. One sees here a wide range of activities, swimming appearing most frequently (12.5 per cent of the pictures) and riding horseback being second in frequency. The total number of times indoor recreation activities were pursued in these 40 pictures was exactly three times as great as the outdoor; 192 in the

TABLE 42

OUTDOOR RECREATIONS OF THE LEADING CHARACTERS IN THE 40 PICTURES

Number of each type of character indulging in each type of recreation and the number and per cent of the pictures in which each type of recreation was shown

Type of Recreation	Number of Characters								Pictures	
	Hero	Heroine	Villain	Villainess	Other Men	Other Women	Group	Total	Number	Per cent
Swimming.........	4	4		1	1	2	1	13	5	12.5
Riding horseback....	3	2				1		6	3	7.5
Picnicking.........	1					1	2	4	2	5.0
Walking...........	2	2						4	2	5.0
Boating...........	1	1						2	1	2.5
Fishing............	1				1			2	1	2.5
Golfing...........					1			1	1	2.5
Hunting...........					2			2	1	2.5
Skiing............	1				1		1	3	1	2.5
Tobogganing.......							1	1	1	2.5
Riding in										
Auto............	5	6	1	1	1			14	6	15.0
Horse-drawn vehicle	1	2	1		1			5	3	7.5
Airplane..........	1	2	1					4	2	5.0
Bus.............	1	1						2	1	2.5
Taxi.............		1						1	1	2.5
Total.............	21	21	3	2	8	4	5	64	20	50.0

former and 64 in the latter. However, when one notes that sports are the highest single item in the newsreels, it is evident that active recreations are not neglected in the total offering. (See Chapter XI.)

In Table 43 are grouped a number of miscellaneous recreational activities, each of which is self-explanatory. Group singing as an activity is surprisingly high. However, an analysis of the nature of the group singing discloses that

TABLE 43

MISCELLANEOUS RECREATIONS OF THE LEADING CHARACTERS IN THE
40 PICTURES

Number of each type of character indulging in each type of recreation and the number and per cent of the pictures in which each type of recreation was shown

Type of Recreation	Number of Characters								Pictures	
	Hero	Heroine	Villain	Villainess	Other Men	Other Women	Group	Total	Number	Per cent
Group singing.......	2	1		1			11	15	11	27.5
European travel.....	2	3	1	1	4	1	1	13	3	7.5
Playing (children) ...	1				8			9	3	7.5
Telling stories.......		1			2			3	2	5.0
Fencing.............	1				1			2	1	2.5
Miniature golf.......					1			1	1	2.5
Watching:										
Football game.....	2	4		1	3	1	4	15	4	10.0
Horse race........	1	1			4	3	2	11	2	5.0
Baseball game.....	1					1	1	3	1	2.5
Bicycle races......	1		1		2		1	5	1	2.5
Card tricks.......		1						1	1	2.5
Dramatic recital...	1	1					1	3	1	2.5
Knife-throwing....							1	1	1	2.5
Military maneuvers		1				1	1	3	1	2.5
Tournament.......	1		1	1			1	4	1	2.5
Wrestling match...							1	1	1	2.5
Total..............	13	13	3	4	25	7	25	90	20	50.0

the majority of the types of group singing represent choral work of groups of soldiers, school singing, etc. In only three cases was there spontaneous singing by a small group, and in two of these incidents the participating members were drunk.

It is interesting to compare the number of times that the characters were seen watching games with the number of times that they themselves participated in the activity. Table 42 shows that 38 times leading characters were seen swimming, horseback riding, walking, and so forth, while Table 43 shows that they were seen watching a football game, a horse race, a baseball game, or other sport 47 times.

Liquor in the Movies

The charge has frequently been made that the movies contain a high proportion of drinking scenes, that intoxication is shown as humorous, that the prohibition law was flouted by attractive characters, and that the harmful effects of liquor and the total results which accrue from it are not shown. Are these charges true?

TABLE 44

USE OF LIQUOR IN THE 115 PICTURES

Comparison of the results of two samples of motion pictures as to the number and per cent of the pictures which contained liquor situations

Type of Situation	The 40 Pictures		The Re-maining 75		Total	
	Num-ber	Per cent	Num-ber	Per cent	Num-ber	Per cent
Pictures containing liquor situations...	37	92.5	53	71	90	78
Pictures without liquor situations...	3	7.5	22	29	25	22

Tables 44 and 45 give us the liquor situations as shown in the pictures analyzed by the schedule sheet and by viewing at the theaters, and the 40 pictures which were viewed at the theater and written up in great detail. The terms used are defined as follows:

Drinking Shown—In this category are placed all situations where liquor is actually drunk by characters, in view of the audience.

Liquor Referred to or Suggested—This includes all references to liquor by any of the characters, either a suggestion to have a drink, reference to some one's else drinking, or a comment of any kind upon liquor. If a character is actually drinking, however, his comment upon liquor at that time is not also included in this category.

TABLE 45

Type of Liquor Situation in the 115 Pictures

The number and per cent of liquor situations of each type as shown by two samples of motion pictures

Type of Situation	The 40 Pictures		The Remaining 75		Total	
	Number	Per cent	Number	Per cent	Number	Per cent
Drinking shown.....	29	73	47	63	76	66
Liquor referred to or suggested.........	27	68	—ᵃ	—	—	—
Display of liquor....	15	38	—	—	—	—
Intoxication shown...	21	53	28	37	49	43

ᵃ The dash (—) indicates that the data were not recorded.

Display of Liquor—Of course if there is any drinking at all shown in the picture, there is necessarily display of liquor, but it is not recorded as such unless there is display of liquor without drinking.

Intoxication Shown—This needs no further definition.

It is evident from these tables that most of the charges brought against the motion pictures from the standpoint of liquor are justified. Two thirds of the 115 motion pictures show liquor being drunk. Intoxication was shown in 43 per cent of the pictures. In the detailed analyses we attempted to discover what proportion of the intoxication was shown as humorous. Of the 21 pictures in which intoxication was shown, in 16 it was depicted as humorous. Further, we dis-

covered that 37 of the 40 pictures, or over 90 per cent, contained liquor situations of some type or other. This means
that liquor may have been referred to, ordered, displayed,
suggested, or drunk. In the 75 pictures the proportion was
71 per cent; in the 115, 78 per cent. This means that a child,
youth, or adult who exercises no selection in his motion-
picture attendance sees or hears some reference to liquor,

TABLE 46

DRINKING BY LEADING CHARACTERS IN THE 40 PICTURES

The number and per cent of pictures in which each type of character
was seen drinking

Character	Pictures	
	Number	Per cent
Hero..	17	43
Heroine...	9	23
Villain..	5	13
Villainess.......................................	3	8
Other men.......................................	17	43
Other women.....................................	5	13
General drinking.................................	5	13

direct or indirect, in three pictures out of four. Further, the
chances are highly favorable that if intoxication is shown,
it will have an element of humor attached to it.

But, it may be asked, is it not important to state who does
the drinking? Is it done by the hero or heroine? The villain
or villainess? Table 46 gives the answer. It must be remembered that this includes only about one tenth of the annual
production of motion pictures and may not represent an adequate sampling. It is evident from these pictures, however,
that much of the liquor drunk by leading characters is con-
sumed by the hero and the heroine.

What of it? It is evident that the prohibition law received
scant support from the producers of motion-picture drama.

Further, the conviction that drinking is universal in the United States must inevitably have received a tremendous impetus from the nature and extent of the drinking shown in motion-picture films.

The deliberate nature of this program is indicated in the following statement by Clarence Brown which appeared in the *Film Daily* for December 4, 1933.

BROWN WOULD BACK FREEDOM OF PRESS

Hollywood—Freedom of the press, now a sharp issue in national politics, is a principle which the motion picture industry should defend to the utmost, according to Clarence Brown, M–G–M director. The interests of pictures and the newspapers are closely allied in this respect.

While the screen does not enjoy the uncensored freedom the press does, it has been able to enjoy what freedom it does have only by vigilance and aggressiveness, declares Brown. If there is any credit due anywhere for the repeal of prohibition, for instance, the screen should have its share.

"When prohibition was in effect, censorship would have forbidden us to present any scene which included liquor," asserts Brown. "We took the position that motion pictures should depict and reflect American life, and cocktail parties and speakeasies were definitely a part of that life. We were able to prevail to a large extent, and I believe that it was the motion picture, showing that in spite of prohibition liquor was an immense factor in American life, that had a great deal to do with changing sentiment on the question."

Over three fourths of 115 motion pictures analyzed contained some sort of liquor situation. Both men and women were involved in the situations.

Tobacco in the Movies

Those interested in methods by which ideas are distributed may be concerned with the use of tobacco in motion pic-

tures. Many believe—and perhaps with good reason—that
attractive screen heroines who smoke cigarettes tend to
cause shifts in attitudes toward this custom. This interest
may relate not only to the use of tobacco but also to the
types of tobacco used, if one may refer to them in this fashion. Table 47 indicates the use of tobacco by the leading
characters. We note that in 26 of the 40 pictures the hero
used tobacco in some form; the heroines in about one third
of the pictures. In other words, in these 40 pictures, there
are about two chances in three of seeing the hero using
tobacco and one chance in three of seeing the heroine using
tobacco. Interestingly enough, the other men smoke tobacco
in approximately the same ratio as the hero.

If one were to compare these figures with smoking by the
general population, it is probable that that of the men might
be somewhat higher, and that of the women somewhat lower.

TABLE 47

USE OF TOBACCO IN THE 40 PICTURES

The number and per cent of pictures in which each type of character
was seen using tobacco and in which there was tobacco used

Character	Number	Per cent
Hero	26	65.0
Heroine	12	30.0
Villain	9	22.5
Villainess	1	2.5
Other men	25	62.5
Other women	10	25.0
Children (under 16)	1	2.5
Total tobacco used	35	87.5

We note in Table 48 the heavy predominance of the use of
cigarettes, which appeared in over two thirds of the pictures,
while pipes and cigars were each seen in less than one third,
and the use of snuff was practically negligible. The predomi-

TABLE 48

The Type of Tobacco Used by Each Type of Character in the 40 Pictures

Number and per cent of pictures in which each type of character was shown using each type of tobacco and the number and per cent of characters using each type

Character	Cigarettes		Pipes		Cigars		Snuff		Total	
	No.	Per cent	No.	Per cent	No.	Per cent	No.	Per cent	No.	Per cent
Hero.............	23	57.5	4	10.0	2	5.0			26	65.0
Heroine..........	12	30.0							12	30.0
Villain...........	6	15.0			2	5.0	1	2.5	8	20.0
Villainess.........	1	2.5							1	2.5
Other men........	26	65.0	9	22.5	12	30.0			24	60.0
Other women......	14	35.0			1	2.5			12	30.0
Children (under 16)			1	2.5					1	2.5
Total pictures.....	27	67.5	11	27.5	12	30.0	1	2.5	35	87.5
Total characters...	82	72.0	14	12.0	17	15.0	1	1.0	114a	100.0

a If one character was seen using two different types of tobacco he was counted as two persons.

nance of cigarettes is brought out even more strongly when we consider the number of persons using each type. Seventy-two per cent were seen smoking cigarettes; 12 per cent were seen smoking pipes; 15 per cent, cigars; and 1.0 per cent were seen using snuff. The leading women characters chose cigarettes to the practical exclusion of all other types. It is interesting to note that pipes were the only type of tobacco not used by the villians.

Summary

The 40 pictures which were analyzed in detail were used for the study of recreations and tobacco and the 115 were used as well in the study of liquor.

In 85 per cent of the pictures the leading characters were seen to be indulging in 28 types of indoor recreations, in 50 per cent they were seen pursuing 15 types of outdoor recreation, and in 50 per cent they were seen engaging in 16 types of miscellaneous recreations 10 of which involved the watching of some sport. *Dancing, having tea, playing the piano, listening to the radio, swimming, auto riding, attending the theater, group singing,* and *watching a football game* were the activities that were shown in 10 per cent or more of the pictures.

Liquor was seen in over three fourths of the pictures. The drinking of intoxicants was depicted in about two thirds of the pictures, intoxication was shown in 43 per cent. The *hero* and the group designated as *other men* did the major part of the drinking, the *heroine* was next in rank, and oddly enough the *villainess* was last.

Tobacco was used in 87.5 per cent of the pictures. The *hero* did the major part of the smoking. The *heroine* smoked more than either the *villain* or *villainess* and the *villainess* tied with *children* for last rank. Almost three fourths of the characters who used tobacco were seen smoking cigarettes.

The use of leisure time is a subject of increasing importance. What patterns for recreations are set up in the movies? Are they ones which the vast audience can imitate? Are they socially desirable?

From the data here presented we see that a large variety of recreations are presented in the movies. Those presented are primarily ones which seem desirable and which might be followed by persons of moderate income. However, the same comment that has been made in connection with clothing is apropos here—the recreations that were portrayed were shown for the most part in expensive surroundings, though the majority of them might have been displayed against a more moderate background. It is true that there was an emphasis on the spectator or non-participating type of recreations, which is probably in conformity with the present recreational status of America.

There is much food for thought in the fact that the use of liquor was shown in many pictures during the prohibition era. What was the responsibility of the movies at this time? Should they have given support to the prohibition law by not showing the use of liquor? Such a question is difficult to answer. Clearly, however, drinking has never been as common in the general population as it is in the movies. It is also interesting to note that the hero and heroine did much of the drinking. Evidently, therefore, a certain degree of attractiveness was connected with the consumption of liquor in the movies.

One can hardly doubt from these figures that the movies are effective in setting up the standards of approved drinking. It is also clear that all the consequences of the drinking of alcoholic liquor are not presented in the movies.

Taking into consideration the types of persons presented, the representation of the use of tobacco is probably a fairly accurate picture of its use in real life. Whether or not it is considered desirable will depend upon one's philosophy as to the purpose of the movies and the use of tobacco.

CHAPTER XI

THE GOALS SOUGHT BY THE LEADING CHARACTERS

THE purpose of this chapter will be to secure answers to the following questions:

1. What are the major goals of the leading characters in the 115 pictures which were analyzed?
2. How are these goals distributed among the heroes, heroines, villains, and villainesses?
3. Are the goals of the attractive characters of a type which merit approval and acceptance as guides to conduct?
4. What shifts in goals are desirable in order to make motion pictures socially acceptable?

The function of education is that of developing in the learner a dynamic philosophy of life. In other words, we aid the learner in analyzing the values of certain goals and we suggest methods for reaching those goals. The motion picture, interestingly enough, does the same thing. Through its characters it shows us what the motion-picture director and the story writer have conceived as a worthwhile life, since they show their characters striving for certain goals. It has been the aim of this analysis, therefore, to study very carefully the goals portrayed in 115 motion pictures.

The significance of this analysis lies in the fact that other investigators in this coöperative study have discovered that the attitudes and techniques shown in the film have a profound effect upon the viewer. Therefore, we may expect that there will be a strong tendency for children and youth to take over the attractive goals and methods found in motion pictures. We can expect that large portions of our population will seek goals shown on the motion-picture screen as commendable. Further, when such persons meet situations in life which are analogous to those they have seen on the screen, we may expect that, other things being equal, they will accept the solution offered in the motion picture. These goals indicate to children and youth those things which popular motion-picture characters find it worth while to achieve.

What goals, then, do the leading characters in motion pictures find worth while?

The method used to determine these goals was to have several persons study the story carefully, view the picture, and then indicate what the principal characters were explicitly trying to achieve. It should be pointed out at the outset that this is a far simpler thing to do in a motion picture than it would be in real life. Nearly every motion picture is built upon a simple theme which relates to the one or two goals of a few leading characters and the ways in which these goals are thwarted by various influences. For example, a young man may have as his goal the winning of the love of a girl. The thwarting influence may be a rival, the parents of the girl, the girl's husband, a brother, differences in social position or economic level, racial differences, lack of money, family responsibility, and so on. Indeed, most motion pictures do have in them two characters whose goal is to win each other's love. We see that one can readily determine what the pictured goals of the various characters are. Whether these pictured goals are the ultimate or final or real goal of the character, we do not know. We cannot go beyond the material which is presented on the screen. The play begins and ends. We must assume that the director has done his best to show us what the characters were striving for and we must take as the goals of the characters those which are explicitly presented in the play.

It should be pointed out that the variation from observer to observer is exceedingly slight on the problem of determining the major goals of each of the characters. The disagreement occurs only on the number of goals given for each character. In other words, one reviewer may give two major goals; another reviewer will give three. There may also be a disagreement on the question of whether they are major or minor goals. This will not affect the accuracy of the report on the occurrence of certain goals, but rather the proportion of the goals of certain types.

Three types of goals are here described: individual, personal, and social. An individual goal is one in which the character is trying to achieve something for himself—he will receive the major benefit of his action. The personal goal is one where he is trying to achieve something, not merely for himself, but rather for a small group, all of whom he knows well. A social goal is one in which the character carries out a line of action the benefit from which will accrue not merely to himself or to a group with whom he is personally acquainted, but primarily to humanity in general.

INDIVIDUAL GOALS

Table 49 indicates the individual goals of highest frequency as discovered in 115 motion pictures. The most striking fact of the table is that *winning another's love* is the most common goal in this group. It was found in 81 of the pictures, or 70 per cent. Leading characters in the following number were actuated by this goal: heroes, 65; heroines, 51; villains, 13; villainesses, 3; other men, 20; and other women, 6. When we consider the fact that *marriage for love* is the second highest individual goal, we readily

TABLE 49

INDIVIDUAL GOALS OF THE LEADING CHARACTERS IN THE 115 PICTURES

Distribution of individual goals according to types, pictures, and character

Type of Individual Goal	Pictures		Number of Goals per Type of Character							Total	
	Number	Per cent	Hero	Heroine	Villain	Villainess	Other Men	Other Women	Group	Number	Per cent
Winning another's love..	81	70	65	51	13	3	20	6		158	18
Marriage for love......	41	36	23	30	4	1	5	4		67	8
Professional and vocational success........	31	27	20	9	1		11	1	1	43	5
Revenge..............	29	25	5	8	10	2	8	2	1	36	4
Crime for gain........	23	20	4	1	19	1	2	1	1	29	3
Illicit love...........	22	19	4	3	11	7	7	3		35	4
Thrills; excitement.....	20	17	7	8	2	3	3	4		27	3
Conquering of rival....	17	15	4		14		1	1		20	2
Financial success......	15	13	5	5	5	1	3	2		21	2
Enjoyment...........	14	12	2	5		2	2	11		22	2
Concealment of guilt...	13	11	1		7	1	4	1		14	2
Marriage for money....	13	11	2	5		1	1	4		13	1
Escape from present life	11	10	6	6			1			13	1
Reformation..........	9	8	6	5						11	1
Self-preservation.......	8	7	2	1	1		1	4	1	10	1
Escape consequences of crime..............	7	6	3		2		2	1		8	.9
Social prestige........	5	4			2		1	3		6	.7
Proof of innocence.....	5	4	4				1			5	.6
Success in sport.......	3	3	2		1		1	2		6	.7
Escape..............	4	3	2	1			1			4	.5
Escape past...........	3	3	1	1			1			3	.3
Publicity.............	3	3	1		1		1			3	.3
Get own way..........	2	2	1	2						3	.3
Desire for easy life.....	2	2	1		1					2	.2
Return home..........	2	2	1					1		2	.2
Romantic ideal........	2	2		1			1			2	.2
Other goals...........			4	4	2		1			11	1.1
Total individual goals..	112	97	176	146	96	22	79	51	4	574	65.0
All other goals........			105	83	9		76	36		309	35.0
Grand total..........			281	229	105	22	155	87	4	883	100.0

see the nature of the individual goals which most commonly affect the leading characters in motion pictures. Indeed it is a rare picture in which either of these two goals is absent.

These data confirm the astute observation of the dramatist Elmer Rice, who writes as follows in his brilliant satire on the movies:

> I spoke of love, and well I might, for love is perhaps the key to the whole Purilian world. Not such love as we know on earth: one dynamic element in our complex lives, with manifold biological, psychic, and esthetic implication; but love as the be-all and end-all of life, love as the sole substance and meaning of life, love as a thing in itself, love universal and all-permeating, without any implication whatever. Such is love in Purilia; and an over-powering thing it is! And the reader must understand that the broad plains and the mountain-ranges, the quiet hillsides and the pebbled beaches, the many-towered cities and the straggling towns, and the hordes of animate creatures who inhabit them, are but the paraphernalia of this eternal, cosmic love.[1]

The fact that *professional success* runs as high as it does gives us light concerning the possible effects of the motion picture in setting up certain types of ambitions among the youth and adults who see motion pictures in which the leading characters seek such goals. In only one picture was *professional success* shown as a goal that had undesirable individual and social consequences. The other pictures paint very clearly the ambition of individuals to do a good job in the line of work which they have chosen. Here are some samples: One hero, a sports writer on a New York paper, wants to write a novel; a heroine, an entertainer in a Havana café, wishes to make enough money to go to Rio, where opportunities are much greater; another hero's goal is to be as good a wagon-train scout as the two old scouts who had literally reared him.

The harmful concomitants of the goals of professional

---

[1] *A Voyage to Purilia*, New York: Cosmopolitan Book Corporation, 1930, p. 87.

and vocational success are no greater than those attendant upon the average individual choice in real life. The movies are derelict, however, in their failure to give an interpretation to professional and vocational success which is adequate for current conditions.

Where the professional success lay largely in the area of financial achievement, this goal was labeled *financial success*. Financial success as an individual goal was found in 15 of the pictures, or 13 per cent. In 6 of these pictures financial success was shown as an unattractive goal. In one picture the elderly husband loses his attractive wife because of his failure to understand her need for laughter and joy, and through his own preoccupation with financial gain. In another the villain exploits religion for money. In the third a man is murdered because he has defrauded his murderer. In a fourth picture the villain purports to be a leader of the people in their uprising against the aristocracy, whereas in reality he is merely lining his own pockets with misappropriated funds. In the fifth picture the heroine encourages men other than her husband to pay attention to her in order to fill the family exchequer. In the last one the villain connives to secure possession of a piece of property owned by the heroine.

It is evident that the pecuniary motive as one of the strong drives of our current civilization will receive little criticism from those who make our movies. This situation, however, is an important one in its social implications. Louis N. Robinson of Swarthmore College says:

I believe that much of our mercenary crime is due to the existence of a false set of values—values which people generally hold. What we who do not belong to the criminal classes believe to be worth while is accepted by them more or less as gospel. If we place a higher value on this rather than on that, so will the criminal group. . . . I insist that as a rule criminals get their idea of values from the rest of us.

The goal which we have seemingly placed above all others is the accumulation of wealth. It is the common goal, the one that is discussed on trains, in hotels and in the newspapers; and it is the one which the criminal, who because he stands somewhat outside of society and can judge us accurately and dispassionately, perceives to be our goal. He accepts it and makes it his own.[2]

Revenge ranks fourth as an individual goal, and is found in 25 per cent of the pictures. Five heroes, 8 heroines, and 10 villains are moved by *revenge*. In only one case out of the 5 was revenge shown as an unattractive goal for the hero; in 5 cases out of the 8 it was shown as unattractive for the heroine. For the entire 36 characters whose major goal is revenge, in 19 cases the goal was presented as unattractive. We see, therefore, that the person who attended all of these movies would have received data on both sides of the question as to whether or not revenge was a worthy social goal. It should be pointed out that the attractive presentation of revenge as a goal is in conformity with the mores of a large number of persons, and the motion pictures have merely reflected in some of the instances the mass sentiment on these matters. In view of the tremendous effect of motion pictures relative to the development of attitudes, thoughtful parents and educators must consider the educational effect of the movies which show revenge as an attractive individual goal.

Crime for gain ranks fifth among the individual goals. It is found in 20 per cent of the pictures. Four heroes are moved by this goal—in 3 cases it was presented as unattractive, in one as attractive. The only instance in which the

---

[2] MacDougall, Ernest D., Editor, *Crime for Profit*, Boston: Stratford Company. 1933, pp. 13–14.

heroine was moved by this goal is unattractive. All of the 19 situations involving the villain with this goal are shown as unattractive.

PERSONAL GOALS

Under personal goals as shown in Table 50 we see that goals dealing with love predominate. *Happiness of a loved one* is found as a goal in 27 per cent of the pictures.

TABLE 50

PERSONAL GOALS OF THE LEADING CHARACTERS IN THE 115 PICTURES

Distribution of personal goals according to types, pictures, and characters

Type of Personal Goal	Pictures		Number of Goals per Type of Character						Total	
	Number	Per cent	Hero	Heroine	Villain	Villainess	Other Men	Other Women	Number	Per cent
Happiness of loved one	31	27	16	6	1		11	7	41	5
Happiness of friend	26	23	9	5			9	8	31	4
Protection of friend	22	19	6	3			16	1	26	3
Protection of loved one	17	15	6	11			2	1	20	2
Success in marriage	16	14	10	9			2	3	24	3
Protection of relative	15	13	4	8			3	2	17	2
Rescue of loved one	14	12	4	8			1		15	2
Success of loved one	12	10	1	11				2	14	2
Rescue of relative	9	8	2	3			3	1	9	1
Happiness of relative	7	6		3			3	2	8	.9
Rescue of friend	6	5	4	1				2	7	.8
Success of friend	5	4	1	1			1	2	5	.6
Family welfare	4	3	3	2			1		6	.7
Atonement	3	3	1	1			1		3	.3
Please parents of loved one	2	2		2					2	.2
Protection of family honor	2	2		1				1	2	.2
Success of relative	2	2	1	1					2	.2
Avenge another	1	1	1						1	.1
Total personal goals	95	83	69	76	1		53	34	233	26.4
All other goals			212	153	104	22	102	53	650[a]	73.6
Grand total			281	229	105	22	155	87	883[a]	100.0

[a] Four individual goals of a group do not show on this table, therefore the sum of the rows does not equal the sum of the columns.

Protection of a loved one is found in 15 per cent, *rescue of a loved one* in 12 per cent. The difference in these two goals lies in the interpretation of the latter as guarding some one from a specific threatened danger. *Success of a loved one* is found in 10 per cent of the pictures.

It is difficult to evaluate the effect upon the viewer of the operation of these personal goals in the lives of their possessors. Certainly, in most cases it is more commend-able to have the consequences of one's acts benefit others than to merely benefit one's self. On the whole, these goals are highly commendable ones, and perhaps the only criticism that can be directed against them is their failure adequately to consider the effect of one's actions outside a limited circle of intimates. Intelligent behavior considers all effects, not merely those which are favorable or unfavorable to one's own immediate group. It must be noted, however, that in these personal goals there is emphasized a high amount of friendliness and kindliness to one's fellow men.

SOCIAL GOALS

Twenty-three pictures stress *performance of duty* as the goal of a leading character. This group is by far the largest one involving social goals. Interestingly enough, however, when we split up these goals we discover that a number of these characters are shown doing their duty as civic, military, or government officials. In some of the pictures there was detected a note of unattractiveness in the goal as developed by the character. For example, in one picture we have listed the warden of a penal colony, who is also the villain, under *performance of duty*. As a matter of fact, this was shown in a very unattractive light. And a school teacher in another picture is listed under *performance of duty* as a motive, yet he is shown as a comical character and we would hardly cite him as one who is likely to secure followers for this type of goal.

Performance of duty is distinguished from *welfare of country* in the following way. A man or woman may be intensely

TABLE 51

Social Goals of the Leading Characters in the 115 Pictures

Distribution of social goals according to types, pictures, and characters

Type of Social Goal	Pictures		Number of Goals per Type of Character						Total	
	Number	Per cent	Hero	Heroine	Villain	Villainess	Other Men	Other Women	Number	Per cent
Performance of duty........	23	20	11	1	2		11	1	26	3
Welfare of country..........	9	8	9	3	1		1	1	15	2
Apprehension of criminal....	7	6	5		1		2		8	.9
Solution of crime...........	5	4	4				4		8	.9
Welfare of school...........	3	3	3	2	1		1		7	.8
To see justice done.........	3	3	1				2		3	.3
Scientific achievement.......	2	2	1			1	2		4	.5
Supremacy of state.........	2	2				2			2	.2
Welfare of mankind........	1	1	1	1					2	.2
Philanthropy..............	1	1	1						1	.1
Total social goals..........	38	33	36	7	8		23	2	76	8.6
All other goals.............			245	222	97	22	132	85	807ᵃ	91.4
Grand total...............			281	229	105	22	155	87	883ᵃ	100.0

ᵃ Four individual goals of a group do not show on this table, therefore the sum of the rows does not equal the sum of the columns.

patriotic, but if the evidence of this patriotism is not definitely a part of his or her duty as a servant of the government in some professsional or official capacity, as soldier, spy, and so on, it would be listed under *welfare of country* but not under *performance of duty*.

Apprehension of criminal is found as a goal in 6 per cent of the pictures and *solution of crime* in 4 per cent. Perhaps most striking of all is the fact that *scientific achievement* is found as a goal only 4 times in the 115 pictures and that *welfare of mankind* appears only twice.

We note here that only 9 per cent of the total goals are social in nature. Further, certain of these goals labeled as social are probably inimical to the best interests of society. The interpretation, therefore, has been a liberal one. It is apparent from these data that children will rarely secure from the motion picture goals of a type that have animated men like Jenner, Lister, Koch, Pasteur, Thomas Aquinas, Jesus Christ, Aristotle, Ralph Waldo Emerson, Plato, Socrates, Grenfell, Edison, Noguchi, Lincoln, Washington, and women like Jane Addams, Frances Willard, Susan B. Anthony, Madame Curie, Clara Barton, Florence Nightingale, Grace Abbott, and Dorothy Canfield Fisher.

It is also apparent that were we to include motivations of the type which actuated these characters, it would mean that we would have to introduce ideas into more pictures. That it might meet with an excellent reception is indicated by the success of certain pictures, the producers of which have had the hardihood to give the audience something to think about. Some examples are "All Quiet on the Western Front," "Journey's End," "Broken Lullaby," "Washington Masquerade," "Street Scene," and "Our Daily Bread."

Producers, on the other hand, will quickly cite good pictures which have been "flops." Their reasoning on this matter, it appears to me, is inadequate. Certainly such books as *The Good Earth*, *An American Tragedy*, *Red Bread*, and *Giants in the Earth*, could not have enjoyed popularity as books unless we had trained our population over a long period of years to demand materials of this type. Certainly we should not wish to stop publishing good books because they don't happen to be best sellers. There is little doubt but that every superior picture that is produced wins additional patrons to the motion-picture theater. Therefore, one realizes that it is exceedingly difficult to draw up the balance sheet of a motion picture. Certainly the relation between the income and outgo on that particular picture is not a satisfactory criterion.

Is it possible that private initiative is not adequate for the production of pictures which have in them satisfactory social goals? It is possible—and if such does prove to be the case, there is a need for subsidy by public funds for the production of satisfactory motion pictures. Indeed we have already made a start in this field. The United States Department of Agriculture produced last year 25 motion pictures, the purpose of which was to increase agricultural efficiency. If it is worth while for the government to subsidize an effort to make two blades of grass grow where one grew before, is it not equally worth while to make two social purposes grow where one grew before?

Certainly the continuance of the development of individual or small-group goals cannot be compared in social effectiveness to the imparting of goals of a social nature. We can expect that the goals which are sought by the leading characters will also be sought by large proportions of our population. This seems a logical conclusion because we can expect that children, youth, and adults who view the picture will tend to find things worth while in life which popular motion-picture stars exemplify as worth while in motion-picture dramas. It is evident that undue emphasis on individual or personal goals is at variance with the views that we are trying to develop in the schools, homes, and churches. Certain of these individual and personal goals shown in the movies, however, are eminently desirable ones.

SUMMARY

The study of goals sought by the leading characters was based on the 115 pictures which were actually viewed. The goals were determined by having persons either observe the picture at the theater or read the observer's report and note what each of the leading characters was explicitly trying to achieve.

The goals were divided into three types, which were defined in the following manner. An individual goal was one in which the character was trying to achieve something for himself— he would receive the major benefit of his action. The personal goal was one where he was trying to achieve something, not merely for himself, but rather for a small group, all of whom he knew well. A social goal was one in which the character carried out a line of action the benefit from which would accrue not merely to himself or to a group with whom he is personally acquainted, but primarily to humanity in general.

Twenty-seven types of individual goals were shown in 97 per cent of the pictures, 18 types of personal goals were found in 83 per cent of the pictures, and 10 types of social goals were found in 33 per cent of the pictures. Sixty-five per cent of all goals were individual, 26 per cent were personal, and 9 per cent were social.

The three most commonly seen goals in each group were: *winning another's love, marriage for love, professional and vocational success* in the individual group; *happiness of loved one, happiness of friend, protection of friend* in the personal group; and *performance of duty, welfare of country*, and *apprehension of criminal* in the social group.

It may be true that the goals which are emphasized in motion pictures are merely a reflection of the goals currently emphasized in our modern world. But here is what Arthur E. Morgan, President of Antioch College, says:

> Our civilization is staggering under the load resulting from commonplace motives at a time when the complexities of life imperatively demand a far higher quality of purpose than ever before.[3]

Surely, if the motion picture has a social purpose, and if it has a social vision, those who are responsible for it cannot be content to have it merely reflect current weaknesses of the social environment. We ought to expect the motion picture to show a better way of living than the average which we find outside the theater. There is so much that is commonplace in life outside the theater, there are so many commonplace motives, so many commonplace activities, so much commonplace thinking, that it seems unfortunate to have a motion picture merely reflect current life. We need to see the screen portraying more of the type of social goals which ought to be characteristic of a decent civilization. We need more often to catch a glimpse of the immortality of great characters who have sacrificed opportunities for personal aggrandizement in order that the larger community might have a fuller measure of life.

[3] Address delivered June 17, 1931.

CHAPTER XII

THE CONTENT OF NEWSREELS

THE newsreel is the educational branch of the theatrical motion picture. The various newsreels bear such titles as: "The Talk of the World," "The Eyes and Ears of the World," and the like. Here indeed is a device for the dissemination of news which is unparalleled in its power. Through the newsreel it is possible for an understanding of new inventions—social and mechanical—to be shared quickly by the 77,000,000 people who attend motion pictures. The newsreel is a device by means of which the population can be made intelligent about the events which are current in this complex and changing world in which we live. How well does the newsreel measure up to the ideal which has been set up for it? The analysis here presented attempts to answer these questions.

The analysis of the content of newsreels presents a different picture from that of the analysis of dramatic materials. First of all, each event is an entity in itself and the fifty or sixty feet of film devoted to such an event have no relation to the topic which follows. Second, conversation of the characters has, in most cases, little to do with the content. The speeches of celebrities are a single notable example. These two factors made us decide in favor of using the synopsis sheets of the producing companies instead of analyzing the newsreels at the theaters. The slight disadvantage of missing some of the significant conversation was more than compensated by the fact that through the method we used we were able to study approximately a year's product of two of the major producing companies.

We decided to confine our analyses to two newsreels, which we shall designate as X and Y. These are released semi-weekly and we studied the output of X covering a period of approximately 59 weeks and the output of Y for approximately 44 weeks. The 118 X synopsis sheets and 87 Y were not dated but, judging from the time of occurrence of the events reported, the approximate range of the X newsreel was from April 1931 to June 1932, and that of the Y newsreel from August 1931 to June 1932. Thus we see that the period from August 1931 to June 1932 is covered by both X and Y, while April, May, June, and July of 1931 were covered by X only.

The description given on the synopsis sheets was similar in form to a newspaper item, with a headline, place line, and brief description of the event, but without a date line. The X sheets also gave the footage of each item, but the Y did not. The number of different items on each sheet (and therefore in each newsreel) varied from 6 to 13 on the Y, with an average of about 9, and from 6 to 10 on the X, with an average of about 8. A brief excerpt from each synopsis follows:

X NEWSREEL

"2-GUN" SLAYER CAUGHT IN DESPERATE BATTLE WITH ARMY OF POLICE

NEW YORK, N. Y.—Sought as the murderer of a policeman and a dance hall hostess, Francis Crowley puts up fight reminiscent of wild west before ammunition gives out and tear gas bombs bring his surrender. Rudolph Duringer, accused of one killing, and Helen Walsh, 16-year-old girl, taken with him.

Y NEWSREEL

JAPANESE BOMBS CREATE HAVOC IN SHANGHAI

Y News gives you a vivid picture of the devastation in the leading city of China in additional films rushed from the Orient by fast steamer and airplane. These are the first sound pictures from the war zone, made in the midst of the Chinese counter attack which retarded the Japanese advance.

METHOD OF CLASSIFICATION

We are next faced with the problem of classification. Our aim was to secure a classification which would readily identify the nature of the content to the layman; in other words, to use what might be called a "common-sense" classification. Therefore, we adopted certain divisions which would make it possible to answer a number of important questions that are being asked about newsreel content, namely: Is more attention given to war than peace? Are current economic conditions being treated in newsreels? Is there a tendency for crime news to be included? Are bathing girls shown more frequently than government officials? Are religious activities ever treated? What does the newsreel show us of the drama of modern industry?

Classifications which had been developed by investigators of the content of newspapers and magazines were consulted and changes made in accordance with the nature of the material and the questions to which we were trying to secure an answer. The following represents the list of categories which was drawn up. Sufficient examples are given under each heading to show their meaning. The number of examples given under each heading has been purposely varied, since some of the categories are self-evident, while others need more illustrations to make their meaning clear.

1. Accidents, Fires, Storms, Wrecks, and Disasters

5,000 MADE DESTITUTE AS RAGING FLAMES
RAZE NATIVE HOMES (Manila, P. I.—Foreign)   X
TORNADO CAUSES DEATH AND RUIN IN THE
SOUTH   Y
PASSERBY KILLED IN GAS BLAST CAUSED BY
WOMAN'S SUICIDE TRY   X

2. Animals, Birds, Fish, and Insects

FELINE QUEENS VIE IN SEASON'S OPENING
THROUGHBRED SHOW   X
WESTERN WINTER DRIVES BUFFALO INTO
SHELTER   Y
HERRING STAMPEDE NETS RICH HAUL FOR
CAPE COD SEINERS   X

3. Aviation (Civil)

BOARDMAN–POLANDO LAND IN TURKEY; SET
NEW NON–STOP MARK   X
GERMANY BUILDS A NEW DO–X (Foreign)   Y
MILLION–MILE FLYING RECORD ACHIEVED
BY PIONEER AIRMAIL ACE   X

4. Beauty Contests

HOLD FIRST STATEWIDE NEGRO BEAUTY
SHOW   X
BATHING BEAUTIES OUT IN FLORIDA   Y
BEAUTY CROWN GOES TO MISS BELGIUM   Y

5. Celebrities

CHEERING THOUSANDS GREET ARRIVAL OF
EX–KING OF SPAIN (London—Foreign)   X
SOVIET ENTHUSIASTS HAIL VISIT OF SHAW
ON HIS 75TH BIRTHDAY (Moscow—Foreign)   X
NATION MOURNS AS JULIUS ROSENWALD
GOES TO FINAL REST   X

INDIA'S MAHATMA BRINGS SPIRIT OF EAST
TO EUROPE (Marseilles—Foreign)   Y

CHARLIE CHAPLIN'S BOYS GO ABROAD   Y

CHARLES M. SCHWAB IS OPTIMIST AT 70   Y

6. Children and Their Activities

CHILDREN'S HOMAGE A TOUCHING FEATURE
OF GOETHE CENTENNIAL (Vienna—Foreign)   X

CAPE MAY BABIES GO ON PARADE   Y

THOUSANDS ACCLAIM COLORFUL ENTRIES
IN NATIONAL BABY SHOW   X

7. Commerce, Transportation, and Industry

NEW TRAIN MARVEL BREAKS RAIL RECORDS
WITH 78-MILE SPEED (Paris—Foreign)   X

PORT OF ALBANY IS NOW OPEN TO OCEAN
TRAFFIC   Y

RECORD SEA WEATHER FORCES QUICK RE-
TURN OF BIG FISHING FLEET   X

8. Conventions, Reunions, Contests, Parades, Festivals,
and Pageants

CHINATOWN GUARDED AS RIVAL TONGS
HOLD ANNUAL CONVENTIONS   X

CHRISTMAS SPIRIT FLOWS OVER ROME (Foreign)   Y

HISTORIC RITES MARK 500TH ANNIVERSARY
OF JOAN OF ARC'S DEATH (Rouen—Foreign)   X

9. Curiosities and Freaks

WEIRD GRAVEYARD SCULPTURE HONORS
DEPARTED KINFOLK   X

PRESENTING FAMOUS GERMAN ECHO (Foreign)   Y

SCIENCE MARVELS AT LEGLESS WONDER   X

10. Dancing

WEST COAST COUPLE OUT TO SET NEW REC-
ORD FOR FLAG–POLE DANCING   X

OAXACA GIRLS DO NATIVE DANCE (Mexico—
Foreign)   Y

DANCERS DO REAL HIGH STEPPING   Y

11. Economic Conditions

LOCAL BUSINESSMEN'S "HELP YOUR NEIGH-
BOR" IDEA AIDS HUNDREDS   X

MACDONALD SURVEYS REICH FINANCES AS
PARLEY NEARS END (Berlin—Foreign)   X

SENSATIONAL GRAIN RISE AIDS JOBLESS AS
FLOUR SALES ROCKET   X

BRITISH AUTHORITY EXPLAINS DROP OF
GOLD STANDARD (Foreign)   Y

WHY U. S. TREASURY ASKS TAX RISE   Y

LEADER IN BUSINESS SEES UPTURN NEAR   Y

12. Educational and Instructive

"BRAIN TEST" DECIDES REFORM POSSI-
BILITY OF PRISON INMATES   X

INITIATION RUSH ENDS IN GORY VICTORY
FOR FRESHMAN COHORTS   X

UNIVERSITY INSTALLS MONSTER TELE-
SCOPE FOR USE OF STUDENTS   X

DR. BUTLER SHARES IN NOBEL PRIZE   Y

CHICAGO EXPOSITION GETS RARE RELICS   Y

CHICAGO U. GOING INTO THE MOVIES   Y

13. Engineering and Scientific Marvels and Inventions

RESORT TO HYDRAULIC MINING TO RECLAIM
$50,000,000 MOUNTAIN   X

GREAT BRIDGE OVER HUDSON RIVER IS OPEN
TO PUBLIC   Y

SUCCESSFUL TRIAL OF "SYNTHETIC WAITER" AMAZES HOTEL MEN   X

14. Entertainment

"BIG TOP" PERFORMERS THRILL CHILD GUESTS AT HOOVER BOX PARTY   X

CONEY ISLAND FEELS URGE OF SPRING   Y

HALL TWINS WIN TITLE OF WORLD'S YOUNGEST ACROBATS   X

15. Exploration and Adventure

FIND RICH RELICS IN EXCAVATING ANCIENT ROMAN METROPOLIS (England—Foreign)   X

AUTHOR EXPLORES WONDERS OF DEEP   Y

NEW GOVERNMENT PARK DISCLOSES RUINS OF ANCIENT CIVILIZATION   X

16. Fashion Shows

EMPRESS EUGÉNIE HITS COUNTRY BY STORM—REGARDLESS   X

AND NOW WE HAVE GIGOLO FASHIONS   Y

COIFFURE FEATHERS TO MATCH GOWNS, IS NEWEST PARIS EDICT   X

17. Government and Civic Officials

PRESIDENT ATTENDS LONGWORTH BURIAL AS NATION MOURNS   X

IL DUCE PRESENT AT CATHEDRAL WEDDING OF AIDE'S DAUGHTER (Foreign)   X

ACCLAIM MELLON AS NEW AMBASSADOR TO COURT OF ST. JAMES   X

BRIAND AND LAVAL, FRENCH LEADERS, HAILED IN BERLIN (Foreign)   Y

THIS MAN PROBABLY WILL LEAD HOUSE IN WASHINGTON   Y

18. Governmental-Political-Civic (Activities)

KING CUTS VACATION IN EFFORT TO AVERT
GOVERNMENT CRASH (Foreign)   X

HOLIDAY GIFT TIDE ENGULFS TIRELESS
POSTAL WORKERS   X

MUNICIPAL GOVERNMENT TURNED OVER
TO FAIR SEX ON LEAP YEAR   X

CONGRESS MEETS AT WASHINGTON IN 72ND
SESSION   Y

REPUBLICANS WILL MEET IN CHICAGO   Y

U. S. INVESTIGATOR BACK FROM HAWAII   Y

19. Music

HERE'S $1,000,000 WORTH OF MUSIC   Y

WORLD PAYS TRIBUTE ON BI-CENTENNIAL
OF NOTED COMPOSER (Austria—Foreign)   X

GEORGE GERSHWIN PLAYS FOR YOU   Y

20. Police and Criminal Activities

6 DIE AND 11 SHOT IN BATTLE WITH THUGS
IN N. Y. STREETS   Y

NATION AROUSED AT REVOLTING KIDNAP-
ING OF LINDBERGH BABY   X

AL CAPONE BEGINS 11-YEAR SENTENCE IN
U. S. PRISON   Y

21. Prohibition and Liquor

BEER FOR TAXATION DEMONSTRATION IS
HELD IN NEW YORK   Y

COAST GUARD NAB FLEEING RUM CREW
AFTER WILD PURSUIT   X

HEAD OF W.C.T.U. TELLS BENEFITS OF
PROHIBITION   Y

22. Religion

REVERENT THRONGS HAIL PROCESSIONAL
OF THE HOLY BLOOD (Belgium—Foreign)   X

CATHOLICS HONOR FIRST PRESIDENT   Y

GHETTO, IN BEE–HIVE OF ACTIVITY ON
EVE OF PASSOVER FÊTE   X

23. Scenic Splendors

FAMOUS CHERRY BLOSSOMS A–BLOOM (Washington, D. C.)   X

JACK FROST ADORNS FISHING SHIPS   Y

IT'S NARCISSUS TIME IN HOLLAND (Foreign)   Y

24. Sports

RECORD THRONG SEES LONDOS PIN STEELE
IN FURIOUS MAT BOUT   X

"FIGHTING IRISH" ARE OUT   Y

AMERICAN NET STARS TAKE LEAD IN
OPENER OF DAVIS CUP FINALS   X

25. War-Army-Navy

NATION STIRRED AT HISTORY'S GREATEST
AËRIAL MOBILIZATION   X

GERMANY HONORS HER WAR DEAD (Foreign)   Y

NEW ATTACK INFLICTS HEAVY CASUALTIES
ON EVE OF TRUCE PARLEY (China—Foreign)   X

26. World Peace

GOVERNMENT SCRAPS SUBS IN ACCORD WITH
DISARMAMENT PACT   X

SIR JOHN SIMON GIVES TALK ON PEACE   Y

LEAGUE OF NATIONS GROUP SAILS IN HOPE
OF ENDING WAR CRISIS   X

The *celebrities* category was one of the first ones which we had to revise. At first, we had placed in it all outstanding individuals, regardless of the causes of their importance. Since this obscured a number of important facts concerning such individuals, the classification was altered, and its scope was diminished greatly in the final sense in which we used the word. We placed in it those individuals who had "made the headlines" in a way that could not be classified in any other fashion. For example, a number of the shots of Lindbergh were placed under *aviation;* pictures of Hoover under *government officials.* A shot, however, of John D. Rockefeller was placed under *celebrities.* It is true that it would have been possible to further classify a number of the celebrities we had, but since the total number of different items was only 22, such a further classification would have added little.

We discovered also that it was necessary to discard a category which we had labeled *interesting and unusual occurrences.* We found that it was receiving too large a proportion of the items and that the identity of many items was being lost through use of this classification. It was therefore dropped and the items formerly placed under it were reclassified.

Another category which was discarded was titled *foreign countries.* It, too, was consuming too large a percentage of items of widely varied character. We thought it desirable, however, to discover what percentages of items were of foreign nature, so we classified them into the 26 categories finally utilized, but indicated their origin by the letter "F." It is possible, therefore, to make certain statements finally about the percentage of the shots which dealt with native and foreign activities.

Table 52 presents the frequency of appearance of foreign items in newsreels.

This table is read as follows: In X newsreel, items which dealt with foreign topics appeared in 99, or 84 per cent of the newsreel. In the same fashion, 81 of the Y newsreel, or 93 per cent, contained foreign items.

This fact of frequent inclusion of foreign items in the newsreels of these companies does not, however, give us any indication of the per cent of the total items devoted to foreign material. This is presented in the second half of the table, which shows that the X newsreel had 188 foreign

TABLE 52

FREQUENCY OF APPEARANCE OF FOREIGN ITEMS IN NEWSREELS

The number and per cent of reels and of items which dealt with foreign countries and with the United States

Type of Locale	Reels				Different Items			
	X		Y		X		Y	
	Num-ber	Per cent	Num-ber	Per cent	Num-ber	Per cent	Num-ber	Per cent
Foreign......	99	84	81	93	188	20	168	22
United States	118	100	87	100	764	80	604	78
Total........	118	100	87	100	952	100	772	100

items out of a total of 952 items, or 20 per cent; while the Y newsreel had 168 foreign items out of a total of 772 items, or 22 per cent.

We see, therefore, that the newsreel is by no means provincial. It does deal to a significant extent with foreign countries and peoples.

We discovered also that several of the classifications were too narrow and that they could be easily regrouped into a classification which did no violence to the items. The resultant group was titled *conventions, reunions, contests, parades, festivals, and pageants.*

The utilization of two categories, *government and civic officials* and *governmental-political-civic (activities)*, may need explanation. We discovered that there were two rather distinct types of newsreel shots dealing with government. The one presented a specific governmental activity; the other merely showed the official himself and presented no content of a governmental, political, or civic nature. For example, shots of Mayor Walker in some foreign country were classified under *government and civic officials*, while a shot of Mayor Walker "at work" was placed under *governmental-political-civic* activities.

When the classification had finally been developed, an attempt was made to discover whether different observers would place items in their proper categories with a high degree of consistency. We discovered that when 100 items were selected and independently classified by two individuals there was a high degree of consistency in their judgments. There is evidence, therefore, that the data which we present are highly consistent, and had other observers been utilized, the items would have been classified in large measure as they are presented here. The validity of the classifications and the accuracy with which they present the data will have to be judged by the reader on the basis of the examples presented in this chapter.

Results of the Analysis

The essential data from the study of the content of newsreels are presented in Table 53. The table is read as follows: Sports news is first in frequency of appearance in both the X and Y newsreels. It appears in 87 of the 118 X newsreels, or 74 per cent, and 82 of the 87 Y newsreels, or 94 per cent. Further, there were 138 different items in the X newsreel dealing with sports and 230 in the Y newsreel. These percentages of the total number of items are 14 and 30 respectively.

The reader will be interested first of all in noting the rank of the items in the two newsreels. The rank correlation

TABLE 53

TYPE OF SUBJECT MATTER CONTAINED IN NEWSREELS

The number and per cent of reels and of items which dealt with each type of subject matter arranged according to frequency of X newsreel

Category	Rank According to Frequency X	Rank According to Frequency Y	Reels X No.	Reels X Per cent	Reels Y No.	Reels Y Per cent	Different Items X No.	Different Items X Per cent	Different Items Y No.	Different Items Y Per cent
Sports	1	1	87	74	82	94	138	14	230	30
Animals, birds, fish and insects	2	12	71	60	15	17	85	9	15	2
War—Army—Navy	3	2	64	54	53	61	83	9	89	12
Aviation (civil)	4	4	52	44	32	37	66	7	42	5
Engineering and scientific marvels and inventions	5	20	47	40	8	9	65	7	8	1
Accidents, fires, storms, wrecks, and disasters	6	16	52	44	12	14	62	6	13	2
Conventions, reunions, contests, parades, festivals, pageants	7	5	43	30	29	33	40	5	37	5
Economic conditions	8	9	40	34	22	25	43	5	26	3
Government and civic officials	9	3	40	34	52	60	47	5	77	10
Curiosities and freaks	10	25	34	29	2	2	43	5	2	.3
Police and criminal activities	11	7	37	31	25	29	42	4	32	4
Governmental—political—civic	12	8	34	29	23	26	37	4	29	4
Religion	13	19	31	26	11	13	33	3	11	1
Educational and instructive	14	14	27	23	15	17	30	3	17	2
Commerce, transportation, and industry	15	18	23	19	11	13	26	3	11	1
Celebrities	16	11	22	19	16	18	22	2	17	2
Prohibition and liquor	17	6	17	14	26	30	19	2	28	4
Children and their activities	18	17	15	13	12	14	15	2	12	2
Entertainment	19	24	13	11	5	6	15	2	5	.6
Fashion shows	20	15	10	8	15	17	10	1	15	2
World peace	21	22	7	6	7	8	7	.7	7	1
Beauty contests	22	23	5	4	6	7	5	.5	6	.7
Exploration and adventure	23	26	5	4	1	1	5	.5	1	.1
Music	24	10	2	2	19	22	2	.2	19	2
Scenic splendors	25	21	2	2	8	9	2	.2	8	1
Dancing	26	13	1	1	15	17	1	.1	15	2
Total			118	100	87	100	952	100	772	100

between the two is +.54, showing that there is a fair degree of similarity between what the two newsreel companies consider important for the spectator to see. Diversities of emphasis appear in the categories *animals, etc.; engineer-*

ing; etc.; accidents, etc.; curiosities and freaks; music; and *dancing.*

Space forbids the extensive discussion of the results of this analysis. The reader will find here data which will merit his careful study. Perhaps the most striking fact brought out is the tremendous emphasis given to sports. In the Y newsreel more than twice as many items dealt with sports as compared to the next most frequently appearing item, *War-Navy-Army* activities.

THE NEWSREEL AND WAR

This item of *War-Navy-Army* activities also merits our attention since it ranks third in the X newsreel and second in the Y newsreel. Since 54 per cent of the X and 61 per cent of the Y newsreel contain shots of such activities we note that the chances are greater than even that one will see some phase of war activity depicted on the screen if he sees either of these newsreels.

A random sampling of the items classified under *War, Navy, and Army* follows:

Y NEWSREEL

1. WAR HEROES MARCH AT EASTON
Notables review brilliant parade of Legionnaires at their thirteenth State Convention.
Sub 1—Charles Engard, retiring State Commander, says farewell to his guests.

2. MUSSOLINI'S MEN CLIMB HIGH
Famous Alpine soldiers of the Italian Army go up into the mountains for their "field" practice.

3. NEW YORK WOMEN HONOR HERO DEAD
D. A. R.'s shaft to unknown Revolutionary soldiers who fell at Saratoga is accepted by Lt. Governor Lehman.

4. GERMANY HONORS HER WAR DEAD
An impressive memorial service held at Munich by Reichswehr recalls end of great conflict.

5. FRENCH STATESMAN DECLARES GERMANY MUST PAY IN FULL
Henry Berenger, Chairman of Foreign Affairs Comm.,voices government's stand. (Editor's Note: This is the most ominous public statement yet made by an important French official on Germany's claim that she cannot continue to pay war reparations. M. Berenger, a former Ambassador to the United States, is a power in France and speaks with authority.)

6. U. S. ARMADA KEEPS IN FIGHTING TRIM
With the Far East aflame, American dreadnaughts concentrate in Pacific for war maneuvers.

7. U. S. ARMY EAGLES STAGE A SHOW
First Pursuit Group fliers spread their wings above Selfridge Field, Mich., in striking maneuvers.

8. JAPANESE BOMBARD KIANGWAN
Y News presents one of the most graphic pictures of actual warfare ever shown on the motion picture screen. Our men were permitted to accompany the Japanese field artillery, landed north of Shanghai after the silencing of the Woosung forts and obtained these remarkable films of the bombardment of Kiangwan village at close range.
Sub 1—Now you will see and hear actual warfare as seldom photographed, the roar of Japan's big guns spelling the doom of everything in range of their deadly hail.

9. JOHN BULL'S NAVY KEEPS IN TRIM
British destroyers practise anti-submarine warfare by exploding depth bombs in the English Channel.

10. U. S. BORDER ARMY KEEPS IN TRIM
Cavalrymen, armored car squadron and plane units conduct a lively "war" all their own near El Paso.

X NEWSREEL

1. ARMY PLANES "ATTACK" MANHATTAN IN GREAT AIR DEMONSTRATION

New York, N. Y.—Gotham's millions are enthralled at maneuvers of 672 daring aviators flying greatest armada in history over the peaks of the metropolis despite adverse weather conditions. Aërial daredevils swoop down on city in huge offensive and "capture" it. A graphic lesson in the practical functioning of one of the nation's greatest defensive arms.

2. NATION STIRRED AS SOVEREIGN DEDICATES GIANT VICTORY ARCH

Genoa, Italy—King Victor Emmanuel unveils memorial to the war dead at brilliant service. Famous fighting legions of army march in honor of occasion celebrating the happy ending of great conflict by presenting handsome work of art by Arturo Dazzi to the Motherland.

3. FEDERALS CAPTURE REBEL CHIEFS AFTER LONG OCEAN PURSUIT

Havana, Cuba—Former President Mario Menocal and Col. Charles Mendieta, leaders of the revolution, are returned to the capital on the flagship of the country's navy and banished to prison. Supporters of President Machado view the historic event with a tremendous enthusiasm, and display confidence in the chief executive to end the revolt despite constant rumors of filibuster parties.

4. NOTABLES PRESENT AT RE-ENACTMENT OF HISTORIC BATTLE

Yorktown, Va.—The sesquicentennial anniversary of the birth of Freedom is marked by the surrender of the British forces under General Cornwallis to the remnant of Washington's Revolutionary army, in a colorful pageant commemorating the event. The scene is portrayed before a gathering of spectators that includes President Hoover, Marshal Petain of France, and General John J. Pershing. Uniforms, guns, and armament employed by the weary detachments in 1781 are again used by the actors taking part in the impressive engagement.

5. JAPAN DEFIES LEAGUE AS WAR CLOUDS LOOM ON
   FAR EAST FRONT

Mukden, Manchuria—The first pictures to reach this country
of the battle zone in the Orient that threatens to disturb world
peace.   Bloody conflict marks the bitter resistance set up by
the Chinese against the policy of her imperial neighbor, who
sends forces into the north country determined to control the
borders in spite of demands made upon it by the League of
Nations and the Kellogg Peace Pact.

6. THRILLED CITY HAILS NEW BRIGADE HEADED
   BY ROYAL GENERAL

Naples, Italy—Under a background of gorgeous rolling hills
that sweep from the Bay up beyond the city's limits, Crown
Prince Humbert parades his new command before the populace
of the community.   The skilled maneuvers of the troops win
the admiration of the new leader and the acclaim of the spectators, who are restrained by the police in their anxiety to crowd
into the path of the soldiers as they march up the historic Via
Caracciolo.

7. MONSTER RED ARMY IN MIGHTY ARRAY ON SO-
   VIET ANNIVERSARY

Moscow, U.S.S.R.—In the greatest display of military strength
in Soviet history, 40,000 armed men and women, and a million
workers parade past the tomb of Nikolai Lenin. The ceremony,
in honor of the 14th birthday of the Bolshevik revolt, is climaxed
by the procession, led across Red Square by Klementi E. Voro-
shilov, War Commissar, and reviewed by Joseph Stalin, the
dictator of the government.

8. GRIM PACIFIC ARMADA SAILS TO PARTICIPATE
   IN HAWAII "MIMIC WAR"

San Pedro, Cal.—The greatest peace-time maneuvers ever attempted by the U. S. Navy bring nine mighty dreadnaughts and
fifty-nine submarines and destroyers to this port, where they
weigh anchors for the southern Pacific seas and the great war
games. The Battle Force sails to assemble at a secret rendezvous,
and it is rumored that it may continue on to the unsettled China

area to protect American interests.   The fleet is manned by
15,000 bluejackets, a magnificent naval array.

Meanwhile, at San Francisco, the crack 30th Infantry and
16th Artillery regiments embark on the transport St. Mihiel to
augment the great concentration of forces in the Hawaiian zone.

9. BURNING AND LOOTING TERRORIZE NATIVES' RETURN AFTER TRUCE

Shanghai, China—With Chapei in ruins, refugees from the
razed city rush through the scenes of desolation back to the
mean places they once called home, as miserable free-booters
dash through the wreckage setting fires without restraint.
Eventually captured by the alert guards, they are dealt summary punishment, as the natives, in a panic of despair, battle
wildly for permission to pass through the lines back to their
pillaged quarters.   A picture that will be indelibly stamped in
one's memory.   Meanwhile delegations from the warring factions
call an armistice at the behest of world powers to settle the
trouble without further bloodshed.   Japanese troops on the
battle front continue to hold their position, as the 19th Route
Army of the Chinese moves westward in retreat after a bitterly
fought engagement lasting five weeks.

10. OLD WAR TANK FEATS THRILL SPECTATORS IN FINAL MANEUVERS

Ft. Geo. G. Meade, Md.—Obsolete but still capable, a regiment
of lumbering iron battle-wagons push over hills and valleys in
their breath-taking drill.   Colonel H. L. Cooper, commander of
the post, reviews the detachment as they thunder through steep
grades, trees, shrubs, houses, and other vain obstacles to these
relentless machines of war which know no barriers.   Improved
field methods have made these land dreadnaughts obsolete, but
in this rigid test they are established as weapons of no mean
threat.

THE NEWSREEL AND PEACE

What about peace activities? Apparently they do not
offer so desirable a field for newsreel shots since they are

found in only 6 and 8 per cent respectively of the X and Y newsreels, whereas the war scenes were found in 54 and 61 per cent, respectively. Only 7 peace items were presented in each of the year's output of newsreels. When we compare this with the amount of space given to war activities we find that there were almost 12 times as many different war items as peace items in the X and 13 times as many different war items as peace items in the Y newsreels. The entire group of peace items is herewith presented:

Y NEWSREEL

1. ENGLAND SUPPORTS "UNITED STATES OF EU-
   ROPE"
Lord Robert Cecil, British League of Nations delegate, endorses the Briand plan.

2. MILITARIST RIOTERS STOP DISARMAMENT MEET-
   ING IN PARIS
Disorder commences after former Premier Herriot opens "peace" gathering.
Sub 1—With the representatives of 30 nations on the platform, speakers are interrupted and lights turned off—Alanson B. Houghton of U. S. howled down.

3. 60 NATIONS MEET ON REDUCTION OF ARMAMENT
This is an historic picture, taking you to Geneva inside the hall where the world conference is in session, the most important attempt nations have made to agree on armament questions. Arthur Henderson, the former Foreign Minister of England, makes dramatic opening plea.

4. WOMEN OF WORLD HAVE THEIR DAY AT GENEVA
Mary Dingman, U. S., acts as spokesman as peace petitions are presented.
Sub 1—Mary E. Woolley, member of U. S. delegation, sees reason for optimism.

5. AMERICA PRESENTS ARMS REDUCTION PLAN AT
   GENEVA
Hugh Gibson, head of U. S. delegation, addresses the conference
of 60 nations.

6. SIR JOHN SIMON GIVES TALK ON PEACE
British Foreign Secretary, at Geneva, reviews grave issues con-
fronting world.

7. FORMER ENEMIES NOW FRIENDS AT GENEVA
   PARLEY
Premiers Tardieu, France, Bruening, of Germany, and Mac-
Donald, Britain, meet.
Sub 1—Ramsay MacDonald voices forcible disarmament plea
at lunch given by press.

X NEWSREEL

1. TURKO–SOVIET NAVAL PACT SIGNED AS RUSS
   UNION URGES PEACE
Moscow, U.S.S.R.—Naval building operations in Black Sea are
halted by treaty that may end chronic uprisings in Near East.
Joseph Stalin urges amity between nations of upset Europe as
signatures are affixed to agreement in historic Grand Theatre.

2. GOVERNMENT SCRAPS SUBS IN ACCORD WITH
   DISARMAMENT PACT
Philadelphia, Pa.—Keeping the London agreement the U. S.
delegates several undersea fighters to the background and
prepares to destroy them. Acetylene torches start to eat away
the L–2, which won honors during the war. But treaties must
be kept and to the junkman's pile go the graceful battle-wagons
from the ocean's bottom.

3. IMPOSING ARRAY OF 100,000 ASSEMBLE TO INVOKE
   WORLD PEACE
Vienna, Austria—Headed by President Miklas, government officials, and ecclesiastical dignitaries, a plea for fraternity in international relations is made, a field mass marking the impressive
ceremony. The thousands in attendance pledge themselves and
the branches and guilds they represent to aid in a settlement of

the upset conditions of Europe. The session heralds a new day on the troubled continent.

4. NEWS PARAGRAPHS
Washington, D. C.—Grandi meets Hoover!—Italy's emissary and President reach accord on arms reduction.

5. NEWS PARAGRAPHS
New York, N. Y.—Collegians meet in anti-war demonstration! Students from 65 countries demand international peace.

6. LEAGUE OF NATIONS GROUP SAILS IN HOPE OF ENDING WAR CRISIS
San Francisco, Cal.—Speeding from Geneva, delegated by the Supreme Council to the scene of the Sino-Japanese hostilities, the diplomats are welcomed by Mayor Angelo Rossi. Count Luigi Marescotti of Italy; General Henri Claudel of France; Lord Lytton of England; Dr. Heinrich Schnee of Germany; and Major General Frank McCoy of the United States depart on the President Coolidge for the Eastern front to arbitrate the differences of the two peoples, confident that their intercession will stop the war flames that are kindling hatred and ravaging cities in China.

7. PEACE SIGNALIZED IN FAR EAST AS JAPAN BEGINS EVACUATION
Shanghai, China—After four months of desperate fighting that brought death to thousands and laid many native settlements in ruins, history closes its pages on the tense crisis, as delegates of the warring factions affix their signatures to an armistice. The clouds of battle blow over and Nippon's expeditionary force prepares to withdraw from the invaded territory. Thousands of marines embark on transports bound for their home-land, heralding the return of peace to this disturbed sector.

THE NEWSREEL AND CURRENT ECONOMIC CONDITIONS

That the newsreels concern themselves with economic conditions is shown by the fact that this item ranks eight in X and ninth in Y. Considerable attention is given to *government and civic officials,* this category ranking ninth in X and third in Y. We see, therefore, that there is a constant tendency for government and civic officials to be shown in newsreels. However, officialdom is more frequently seen on the screen than are the differentiated activities—*governmental-political-civic.* This group ranks twelfth in X and eighth in Y.

The extent of enlightenment on economic conditions which one is likely to get from viewing newsreels can perhaps be best gauged by the following descriptions of sample items classified in this category.

Y NEWSREEL

1. PRESIDENT MAKES ECONOMY PLEA TO THE NATION
Addressing the convention of the American Legion in Detroit, Mr. Hoover asks America to take leadership in easing world financial tension.

2. WILL SELL HERSELF FOR $10,000
Mary Clowes, a waitress, of New Eagle, Pa., offers to wed for money to care for her destitute parents.

3. HOW UNCLE SAM IS TO AID BUSINESS
Senator Walcott author of bill creating $2,000,000,000 reconstruction board, tells Federal financial plans.

4. CAMPAIGN OPENED AGAINST HOARDING
New Sec'y of the Treasury Ogden L. Mills explains movement started by President Hoover.

5. BALANCED BUDGET IS PROMISED
Congressman Canfield of the 4th Indiana District gives the details of his work at Washington.

Y NEWSREEL

1. MOBILIZE GUARDS TO QUELL DISORDER AT MINE STRIKE SCENE
St. Clairsville, Ohio—State police gather to prevent outbreak

as woman and children join picket lines, imploring others to join them in their fight. The miners have walked out and laid down terms demanding that living conditions improve before they return to work. Many refuse to join them and labor organizers have been arrested for exhorting employés to quit their jobs. To keep things peaceful and to spare bloodshed the police keep a watchful eye on conditions in the coal regions.

2. HUNGRY BEGGAR MOB STONES RICH ESTATE IN FOOD DOLE DEMAND

Calcutta, India—Unable to restrain the impelling pangs of starvation, the angry tattered horde overflows the barrier separating one of the city's richest families from the outside world. Through the gates the excited throngs swarm and request aid as they over-run the vast grounds. Meeting the threat with an issue of food the crowd is routed, and the tenants of the place are spared.

3. RED HORDES MEET IN NATIONAL CAPITAL AS 72ND CONGRESS OPENS

Washington, D. C.—Unable to rouse the dander of the solons as this history-making session gets under way, the "hunger marchers" from every section of the country parade up Pennsylvania Avenue for a call at the White House. But the presence of police and secret service men induces an orderly meeting. Relief agencies hand out coffee and rolls and the Communistic belligerents remain quiet, as the Democratic House of Representatives elects John Garner, from Texas, to the post of Speaker.

4. FOOD AND FUEL GIVEN JOBLESS AS WAGES IN NEW CIVIC WORK PLAN

Grand Rapids, Mich.—Under the direction of City Manager George W. Welsh, an unique method of dealing with the unemployment problem has been successfully introduced in this community, by which the worker and the city benefit. Hundreds of idle men are employed on highway and street improvement projects for which they receive supplies from the municipal relief stations. The profits from using such labor are turned back into further civic improvements.

5. TROOPS DESPATCHED TO QUELL DISORDERS AT MINE STRIKE ZONE

Cadiz, Ohio—Unrest among workers in the soft coalfields of the Hocking Valley and Sunday Creek sections is aggravated by threats of operators to put non-union labor on the job. Massed movements against the mines are organized by the dissatisfied hands, and National Guard units are rushed into the walk-out area to maintain order and uphold the law. TNT charges, planted in trees, reap a toll of casualties. Armed soldiers take up strategic positions to restrain the maneuvers of the men. The supreme sacrifice is made by several as the grievance over pay warms into a tragic commercial war.

THE NEWSREEL AND LIQUOR

The data in reference to prohibition are interesting. It will be noted that there were 28 items in the Y newsreel and 19 items in the X newsreel. The character of these items offers an interesting reflection on the bias which appears there. In order that the reader may see this bias for himself, we have included here descriptions of all liquor items appearing in both newsreels:

It will be noted that only 3 out of these 28 items, No. 14, 19, and 21, are emphatic in presenting the dry point of view. An additional 3 items dealt with prohibition enforcement, Nos. 3, 11, and 16 making a total of 6 dry items out of the 28.

Y NEWSREEL

1. SENATOR BINGHAM WANTS BEER

Connecticut statesman for legalizing 4 per cent brew to speed return of national prosperity.

2. U. S. WOMEN WETS MOBILIZE FORCES

Opponents of Prohibition hold Detroit convention under the leadership of Mrs. Chas. H. Sabin.

3. UNCLE SAM SEIZES CHRISTMAS CHEER WORTH $500,000
Customs men put damper on New York's holiday joy by big booze haul.

4. PROHIBITION MEANS NOTHING HERE
Rhine maidens of German wine district participate in grape harvest fête as they have for centuries.

5. PROHIBITION FOES STORM CONGRESS
Fred G. Clark, commander of the Crusaders, presents wet petition on the Capitol steps to Senator Bingham.

6. PROHIBITION HASN'T HIT FRANCE YET
Wine shop in The Halles, big Paris market, offers free drinks for all when new vintage comes in.

7. "LITERARY DIGEST" POLLS U. S. AGAIN
Dr. William Scaver Woods explains the mighty job it is to get views of 20,000,000 people upon Prohibition.

8. CONGRESS TO VOTE ON DRY LAW
Representative LaGuardia, New York, hails completing petition of members which compels consideration.

9. HERE'S ANOTHER OF PROHIBITION'S WOES
Dizzy barmaids in popular Berlin café demonstrate what we are deprived of in Land of the Dry.

10. GENE TUNNEY JOINS FIGHT ON DRY LAW
Retired ring champion is welcomed to the ranks of "crusaders" in N. Y. by Commander Curtin.

11. BEER FLOWS FREELY IN CHICAGO!
But don't get excited, it is all under the eyes of dry raiders at $75,000 plant said to be Al Capone's.

12. HAVANA TOURISTS WELCOME 1932
Joy is unconfined at famous Montmartre as New Year descends upon Americans sojourning in damp Cuba.

13. SENATE COMMITTEE FAVORS BEER
Metcalf, Rhode Island, and Bingham, of Connecticut, lead in the movement to bring brew back.

14. "DRYS" TRIUMPH IN CONGRESS
Representatives vote down State liquor control plan—Blanton, Texas Democrat, voices Prohibitionist view
Sub 1—Beck, of Pennsylvania, and Linthicum, Md., led the "wets."

15. EXTRA! FREE BEER! BUT DON'T CROWD
For it's in Germany where the cafés give away their stock in strike against high government tax.

16. UNCLE SAM NABS $300,000 IN RUM
Cargo of a seized collier, the Maurice Tracy, finds unexpected destination at New York Army Base.

17. WOMEN WETS MAKE DRIVE ON CONGRESS
Mrs. Charles H. Sabin leads her anti-Prohibition forces from all parts of the country to steps of the Capitol.
Sub 1—Phyllis Thompson, N. Y., speaks for débutantes opposed to dry law.

18. WHERE HOLIDAYS MEAN BEER
No one goes thirsty when good people of Munich, Bavaria, get together on St. Joseph's Day.

19. HEAD OF W.C.T.U. TELLS BENEFITS OF PROHIBITION
Mrs. Ella Boole, president of women's dry society, grants first interview.

20. WETS OUTNUMBER DRYS 3 TO 1 IN DIGEST POLL
Result of canvass of nation on Prohibition announced by W. C. Roberts, editor.

21. DRYS STILL CONTROL U. S. SENATE
Sheppard, of Texas, again leads fight for Prohibition defeating wets' attempt to legalize 2.75 beer.

22. BEER FOR TAXATION DEMONSTRATION IS HELD IN NEW YORK
Mayor Walker leads 100,000 citizens in all-day parade for Prohibition reform.
Sub 1—And still they come far into the night.

23. WOMAN WETS OPEN NATION-WIDE DRIVE
Mrs. John S. Sheppard and her society assistants start Repeal
Week in New York with open-air meetings.

24. MAYOR CERMAK AIDS WOMEN'S WET DRIVE
Chicago's Chief Executive endorses local campaign of Mrs.
Chas. H. Sabin and leaders of society.

25. WET CANDIDATES WIN IN OHIO
Attorney General Bettman, nominee of Republicans for U. S.
Senator, tells why he is opposed to Prohibition.

**26. REPUBLICANS MEET AT CHICAGO TO NAME
HOOVER**
Senator Dickinson of Iowa stirs convention delegates with praise
of President.
Sub 1—Nicholas Murray Butler, of New York, leads fight for
dry law repeal plank.

**27. JOHN D., JR., JOINS WETS DEMANDING DRY LAW
REPEAL**
Mr. Rockefeller reads his letter to Dr. Butler which surprised
entire country.

28. 2,500,000 WETS JOIN FORCES TO FIGHT DRY LAW
Mrs. Chas. H. Sabin leads in a United Repeal Council headed
by Pierre du Pont.

X NEWSREEL

**1. GAY CITIZENS TEST "EIN STEIN" THEORY AS
BREW SEASON OPENS**
Munich, Germany—Populace stages festival to celebrate new
run of famed Salvator beer in city where lager drinking is an
art and a virtue. Songs, dances and street parade feature vast
picnic, with hot frankfurters and roast spring chicken as relishes
for celebrated beverage.

2. NEWS PARAGRAPHS
Juarez, Mexico—American distiller opens plant below border!—
Introduces new process to age certain beverages banned in U. S.

3. NEWS PARAGRAPHS

Vincennes, France—Wine-market workers hold annual key tourney!—M. Farge is new champion after thrilling barrel sprint.

4. NEWS PARAGRAPHS

Atlanta, Ga.—Anti-Volstead disciple receives just desserts!— Folly of alcohol demonstrated in graphic scenes.

5. WINE–BRICK MAKERS CARRY ON IN FACE OF DRY LEGAL PROBERS

San Francisco, Cal.—Workers continue the manufacture of precious pressed fruit juice concentrate cubes, which, if the purchaser is not careful, may ferment and become beverages that will give the arid forces evidence for the impending court tilts. Shipments far exceeding 50,000 gallons are daily being sent to the eager eastern markets, as factory hands rush process to meet the heavy demands.

6. TRADITIONAL RITES FEATURE ARRIVAL OF NEW VINTAGE CROP

Vienna, Austria—Introduced in the 17th century by Emperor Joseph II, an ancient custom is revived to stimulate interest in the grape industry. The vineyard guard loads a cask on a beautifully decorated carriage and invokes the happy practice of dispensing drinks to the neighborhood. When the barrel is empty it is again filled with the latest brand of wine and passed out until everybody has passed out.

7. VETS DEMAND BEER AS HOOVER PLEADS AGAINST CASH BONUS

Detroit, Mich.—Arriving at this city the President is hailed by millions, eager to catch a glimpse of the chief executive, and to hear the message he brings to the opening of the American Legion convention. A respectful audience at Olympia Hall listens as the nation's leader warns the Legionnaires against over-taxing the government treasury. When his appeal is concluded, an outburst urging the return of legal brew sweeps over the crowd. The annual session gets under way with a parade in which every state in the union is represented.

8. COAST GUARD NAB FLEEING RUM CREW AFTER WILD PURSUIT

Stapleton, N. Y.—After a thrilling five-mile chase, the enforcement squad captures "Baldy" Jim Deering, notorious king of rum row, and a dangerous band of smugglers. Unmindful of the warning issued by the government men, the bootlegger puts his swift speedboat to sea and attempts to elude his pursuers. His stubborn resistance is met with shell-fire, the gang is caught, and the cargo of illicit liquor confiscated. One of the most remarkable action pictures ever caught by the camera.

9. NEWS PARAGRAPHS

Paris, France—Aged waiters hold annual Wine Race!—Veteran, 65, annexes honors in Montmartre classic.

10. FEDERAL RAIDERS NAB RECORD LIQUOR CARGO AND CREW OF 60 MEN

Brooklyn, N. Y.—A surprise attack from shore and water by Prohibition Enforcement agents nets the Raritan Sun, a $750,000 oil-tanker, and a $350,000 haul of contraband rum. Under the guise of a registered fuel ship, the boat makes port, almost unsuspected, but the government men are on the job as soon as the landing of the load starts. So swift and precise is the action of the officers, that the bootleggers are caught unawares, and surrender, without resistance, the rich shipment from the 12-mile limit.

11. NEWS PARAGRAPHS

Havana, Cuba—Wine-inhalers hold "capacity contest!"— Signor Felix Paul downs 3 quarts in one setting.

12. STREETS FLOW WITH BEER RIVER AS POLICE RAID GARAGE HANGOUT

Chicago, Illinois—Halsted Street is swamped with a strange fluid in these days of the Prohibition era. A surprise raid nets agents under Administrator A. E. Aman, 537 barrels of banned brew. The cache discovered, the dry sleuths waste little time in putting an end to the illicit liquid. Armed with mallets and pegs Federal men jam in the bungs and flood the highway and gutters with $30,000 worth of amber brew, as the Windy City's parched gullets moan and wail.

13. SUDS FLOW AGAIN AS U. S. RENEWS WAR ON GANGSTER BEER KINGS

Chicago, Ill.—Led by Deputy Prohibition Administrator Elliott Ness, the raiders demolish a brewery said to belong to the chain operated by Al Capone. Vats, brewing the unmentionable liquid are found, and workers, wheeling scores of barrels of beer to the street, dump the amber fluid into the gutters. Illicit beverages valued, according to those in charge, in excess of $80,000, are totally destroyed.

14. HOBOES SHUN BOWERY DIVES TO SIP BREW AT PHILANTHROPIST'S BAR

New York, N. Y.—Passing up the potent potions in speakeasies, the trampers of the world-famous street beat a path to the door of Urbain Ledoux to put his 3-cents-a-glass concoction to a rigid test. The approving word sweeps up and down the lane of unfortunates and the "Growler" is rapidly filled to overflowing with thirsty throngs. While quenching and satisfying, the suds lack dynamite, but they fill the bill as the boys while away the moments waiting for prosperity.

15. JOYOUS NATIVES HAIL FIRST LOT OF FAMOUS "SALVATOR" BREW CROP

Munich, Germany—The great Bavarian industry reveals the 1932 début of the concoction of the country's best masters of the art. Their efforts are hailed by throngs from all parts of the world, who flock to this capital of fine tap-beer in droves, eager to quench their thirst on the renowned amber fluid. Quaint customs, traditional with this picturesque pageant of color, are revived as the spirit of hilarity sweeps over the community. One of the oddest and most interesting pictures seen on the screen in recent years.

16. DRY LAW REPEALED! GOVERNMENT TO SELL LIQUOR FOR REVENUE

Helsingfors, Finland—Happy-hic-days are-hic-here again. Thirsty thousands pour into the restaurants, cafés and night clubs of the nation as the 12-year-old Prohibition Law is scrapped and the sale of strong beverages is put into the hands of the country's rulers. A last minute threat of an embargo by innkeepers to combat price inflation is adjusted and fresh stocks of imported spirits are offered to the public. The bootleggers, kings of the rum trade since 1919, dry up and take their place in the republic's history—already just a memory.

17. NEWS PARAGRAPHS
Portland, Ore.—Home-brewers hold tourney to decide bottle-capping king!—Winner sets new record of 9 seconds.

18. GOTHAM APPLAUDS AS 150,000 MARCH IN GREAT
    BEER DEMONSTRATION
New York, N. Y.—Behind the jaunty strides of Mayor Jimmie Walker, business leaders, international figures, stenographers, society matrons, and clowns parade down Fifth Avenue advocating the adoption of laws to return the amber beverage with a taxation provision. Another estimated 2,000,000 persons observe the outpouring. Men and women bearing banners proclaiming their prejudices fill the streets from noon until nightfall with an almost endless line of humanity. The most sensational spectacle the city has seen for 40 years.

19. SUDS FLOW AS "FEDS" DESTROY 7 CARLOADS OF
    ILLICIT BEVERAGE
Newark, N. J.—U. S. Department of Justice laborers take free and lusty swings at the bungs in 1800 barrels of confiscated illegal amber fluid, and the government warehouse almost flows off its foundation as the golden river wanders toward the sewer. Fearful that the precious containers might again find their way into bootleggers' hands, the agents cart the carefully charred casks off to the city refuse pile and burn them. The end of a million foaming steins of bubbling brew.

Two of these 19 items from the X newsreel, Nos. 4 and 14, might be considered as presenting the dry point of view, although not very vehemently, and 5 more, Nos. 8, 10, 12, 13, and 19, dealt with enforcement of prohibition, a total of 7 dry items. It will be noted that in a total of 19 items dealing with liquor, the X newsreel presented 5 dealing with prohibition enforcement, as contrasted with only 3 enforcement items out of the larger total of 28 Y newsreel items dealing with liquor.

Suggested Improvements

A statement of the quality of the offerings in these various fields would be a valuable adjunct to this quantitative study. It has not been made a part of this study but demands attention from those who wish to further scrutinize the contribution of the newsreels.

Conclusion

One gets the impression from these newsreels that very little inventiveness and ingenuity are utilized in their construction. They are made according to a formula which, as far as the writer can determine from his own experience, has changed little in the last fifteen years. Further, they omit many interesting and significant aspects of human living which lend themselves to motion-picture photography.

We have noted, for example, that there is great variance in emphasis in reference to a number of topics, while certain topics are omitted.

What possible additions might be made which might interest patrons and which are not now commonly found in motion pictures? The topic of health apparently has not received adequate consideration in motion pictures. It is a topic which is of great interest to well-educated and poorly educated people alike. A number of events dealing with health could be photographed that would be of inestimable value and interest to the public.

Another field of interest almost never found in these newsreels is that of psychological and vocational guidance. There are a number of generalizations in these fields which might be appropriately introduced in a short space of time.

There is no reason, for example, why such a man as Dr. Robinson of Yale might not give a short illustrated talk dealing with the dangers of quack vocational guidance experts. Still another phase of psychology which might be of interest to a great many movie-goers would be short shots dealing with child clinics. For example, a short shot of a nursery school, a short talk by such an authority as Arnold Gesell, demonstrations of psychological testing, would interest many.

In the field of engineering and invention there are areas which are greatly undeveloped. The automobile is one of the most interesting reading topics for adults. And yet we rarely see any scientific demonstration of the automobile or how it works. Through animation it would be possible to show a number of very interesting phases of human life as it relates to the automobile.

In the earlier phases of the development of motion pictures we were treated to a number of so-called educational reels dealing with the manufacture of various types of goods. There is a possibility that a number of these shots might be shortened to make them fit into the newsreel. The writer suggests views of a number of the following items which have dramatic and educational value and which seem legitimately to demand a place in our current newsreels: the drilling of oil wells, the operation of a Jacquard loom, a shot of various operations in a shoe factory, a shot in the assembly room of a large motor company, scenes from a radio station.

Another area which is wholly undeveloped would be short shots of tastefully decorated homes. These might be in color and give to the millions of movie-goers a glimpse into the homes of persons who evince good taste in the selection of furniture and other items of home decoration.

The producers of newsreels may object to some of the suggestions that are presented here. Some of them may prove unworkable; however, one gains the impression from the study of these newsreels that initiative and ingenuity are often lacking. Therefore, the experimentation seems to be desirable in the light of the facts that have been presented.

Summary

The synopsis sheets for approximately a year's production of newsreels from two companies were examined and classified. The classifications are defined by examples of the items that were included under each category. Reliability of the classification was checked by having a second reader independently classify a sample of the items.

As to the categories treated by the two companies a fair degree of relative agreement was found, the rank correlation being +.54. There were wide differences, however, in the per cent of items devoted to each category.

Roughly one fifth of the items were devoted to foreign news. Twenty-six categories were defined. Items dealing with sports were found to be first in rank of frequency for both companies; 14 per cent of the items for X and 30 per cent for Y dealt with this topic.

War-army-navy; civil aviation; conventions, etc.; government and civic officials; economic conditions are some of the categories which ranked high with both companies. *Scenic splendors, exploration and adventure,* and *world peace* are some of the categories which received a low rank with both companies. *Prohibition and liquor,* which are interesting in the light of the recent repeal of the prohibition law, ranked seventeenth in the X newsreel and sixth in the Y.

The content of the newsreel deserves favorable comment.

We ought to be highly gratified that out of the 26 classifications used, those items dealing with economic conditions ranked eighth in the yearly output of X, and ninth in Y's output. Further, those dealing with government and civic officials, we remember, ranked ninth in the X and third in the Y. Further, a third classification which dealt with governmental, political, and civic affairs in general ranked twelfth and eighth respectively.

Many critics of the newsreel comment unfavorably on the extensive emphasis on sports. This overemphasis, if it be such, is probably due to several factors. First, a belief that the public enjoys them; second, the spectacular nature of the sports which lend themselves readily to photographic representation; and third, the relative ease of securing such materials. The writer believes that the newsreel companies are mistaken in their judgment regarding the interest of the public in sports.

Both *peace* and *prohibition* fare badly at the hands of these newsreel companies. The ratio of total peace items to war items in the combined totals of both companies was approximately 1 to 12. The ratio for "dry" items to "wet" items was 1 to 4.

CHAPTER XIII

A SUMMARY

EACH chapter has summarized the significant data on the motion-picture content dealing with major themes, locales and settings, the leading characters, clothing worn, circumstances of meeting and lovemaking, sex, marriage, romantic love, crime, recreations, liquor, tobacco, vulgarity, goals of leading characters, and content of the newsreel. These summaries have certain meaning as they stand alone. But the total significance of all the findings remains to be discussed. Just what does this collection of data on the content of motion pictures mean?

The writer professes no special insight into the fundamental generalizations that can logically be drawn from these data. He has, however, a certain obligation to indicate what they mean to him, however fallible that judgment may be.

Perhaps the most important conclusion concerning these data is the fact that in large measure the characters, the problems, and the settings are remote from the lives of the persons who view them. (The content of the newsreel, however, is an exception to this rule since it frequently deals with the realities of life.) This remoteness is seen in the emphasis placed on romantic love, a problem which nearly all individuals must meet and face in some way, but not in the manner or to the degree indicated in the motion pictures on which we have presented data. It is seen also in the emphasis on wealth and luxury, which serves neither

224

to point a desirable ideal nor to offer methods by means of which the mass of the people can attain that ideal.

Why does the movie deal with unreality? I believe that most persons would agree that the majority of motion-picture habitués secure there an escape from much that is drab, dull, and routinized in modern life. Many people obtain indirectly at the movies what others in the more economically favored groups obtain directly. A study made by the *Literary Digest* at Zanesville, Ohio, showed that there was an inverse relationship between the possession of a telephone (a good index of income) and the statement of motion pictures as one's most interesting hobby.

The contribution that the motion picture has made to such groups must not be underemphasized. A noted critic of the arts has stated, for example, that it is the function of the arts to make life more tolerable. As this relates to the motion picture, however, several facts ought to be remembered. First, drugs are of value when nothing can be done for the patient except to relieve him of pain. Drugs, then, make the pain more tolerable. But we must remember that illness and unhappiness do respond to therapeutic treatment, and drugs should not be resorted to as a substitute for a surgical operation. The good life is no longer a dream which can only be wished for. We now have at hand the machinery for making it a reality. This machinery for changing our current civilization is not commonly shown in the movies.

The motion picture should always play a significant rôle as an instrument of diversion. It must be remembered, of course, that our mental hygienists and physiologists have not yet clarified that concept for us. We must ask, therefore, of these pictures of diversion: "From *what* to *what?*" "Little Women" or "All Quiet on the Western Front" may give us that feeling of diversion, of recreation, far better perhaps than meaningless escape drama.

Further, any well-balanced motion-picture diet must include not only sense but nonsense. It must be remembered, therefore, that there is an art of nonsense just as there is an art of sense. Most of us can appreciate the following poem by Mary Carolyn Davies, which appeared in the *Saturday Evening Post*.

> "Please don't uplift me when I go
> To see a moving-picture show.
> I don't pay cash, or chisel passes,
> To hear about the toiling masses.
> I sort of think the world's O.K.
> If there is something, as you say,
> Rotten in Denmark—then just bury it.
> Don't tell me of the proletariat,
> Or Russian peasants buying tractors.
> I want to watch the movie actors.
> I want to see the villain get
> His just deserts. The Soviet
> Is something that I'd rather miss,
> Of evenings, than the fade-out kiss!" [1]

The motion picture, however, has a very definite and serious rôle to play in the political, economic, and artistic education of the people. Certain of this material will be indirectly presented through the dramatic motion picture. However, a significant portion of it ought to be developed through the newsreel. Further, we must get away from the notion that to be educational is to be dull. Former President Harper of the University of Chicago could teach Greek as though it were a series of hairbreadth escapes. If he could do this, then the motion-picture industry ought to

---

[1] "These Russian Films," *Saturday Evening Post*, November 15, 1930.

be able to take the events of the day, or past events, and dramatize them in a gripping and interesting fashion.

But when we discuss the unreality of films, their inaccuracy, their overemphasis, we still have failed to consider a truly important problem. The writer estimated that in 1929 of the total audience of 77,000,000 people attending motion pictures, 2,000,000 were under 7 years of age, 9,000,000 were from 7 to 13 inclusive, and 17,000,000 were between 14 and 20 years of age inclusive. It is in reference to this large group of children and young people that we must apply these findings of motion-picture content.

In 1930 15.0 per cent of the films dealt with sex, 27.4 per cent with crime, and 29.6 per cent with love. Certainly for the 11,000,000 children under 14 years of age the sex pictures have little value and may in many cases contain a good deal of harm. Even if the data in them are accurate and properly balanced, sex pictures are clearly not the type which children of this degree of immaturity should see. In the same fashion the 27.4 per cent of crime pictures seems to be an overbalanced diet as far as children are concerned. Certainly some of the Westerns which include crime as a major theme may not be harmful to children. Some of them are doubtless valuable. However, when one notes the types of crime that are detailed on page 138, it is obvious that much of this material ought not to be the weekly diet of impressionable children.

The same criticism can be applied to love pictures as a diet for children. Doubtless certain of these pictures of romantic love are commendable for youth; nevertheless there is little in them that makes them desirable for children.

It is unnecessary to repeat here the statements made

concerning the excessive amount of violence shown on the screen. We cannot expect children and young people to develop an appreciation of non-violent methods of settling a dispute if they are constantly subjected to a weekly parade of crimes and violence on the screen. Perhaps the most effective way for the parent, the educator, or the religious worker to evaluate the content of motion pictures in terms of child and youth needs is to consider the objectives of the church, the home, and school on the one hand, and the content of the motion picture on the other. If this is done one sees readily that at certain points these three agencies receive aid from the motion picture. However, far too often the objectives of the motion picture are inimical to those of the church, the home, and the school. If these three agencies wish to conserve what they are doing they must increasingly study not only what the motion picture is doing to the immature, but also the influence of other agencies that are making the American public mind.

Throughout our discussion of motion-picture content we have seen that the motion picture errs not only in what it includes and excludes but also in an over- and under-emphasis of certain elements. The answer to the problem of improving motion-picture content seems to be in terms of effecting a more desirable balance. Some of the elements which have been stressed in the past should receive much less stress; some should be eliminated. Other elements which have been neglected should be given much emphasis.

A balance sheet for the movies follows. On the left hand side are listed those elements which this study has shown to have been emphasized and overemphasized in the past. On the right hand side are listed some elements which, in the opinion of the writer merit much more attention than they have received.

BALANCE SHEET FOR MOTION-PICTURE CONTENT

The following aspects or problems have received attention, sometimes excessive, in the motion pictures.

The following aspects or problems have received scant attention in the motion pictures.

Life of the upper economic strata	Life of the middle and lower economic strata
Metropolitan localities	Small town and rural areas
Problems of the unmarried and young	Problems of the married, middle aged, and old
Problems of love, sex, and crime	Other problems of everyday life
Motif of escape and entertainment	Motif of education and social enlightenment
Interest appeal to young adults	Interest appeal to children and older adults
Professional and commercial world	Industrial and agricultural world
Personal problems in a limited field	Occupational and governmental problems
Comedy foreigner such as the dumb Swede	Representative foreigner such as the worker, business man, farmer
Diverse and passive recreations	Active and inexpensive recreations
Individual and personal goals	Social goals
Variety of crimes and crime techniques	Causes and cures of crime
Emphasis on the romance and unusual in friendship	Emphasis on the undramatic and enduring in friendship
The "lived happily ever after" idea following an unusual and romantic courtship	Happy marriages shown as a result of companionship and careful planning
Physical beauty	Beauty of character
Emphasis on physical action	Increased skill in analysis of motives and portrayal of character
Sports and trivial matters frequently shown in newsreels	World news of an intellectual and perhaps undramatic type, results of scientific findings, pictures of real conditions in the different parts of the world.

We need films for children and youth. They have been the innocent victims of escape movies made for tired, jaded adults. This does not necessarily mean plays in which children take the leading rôles. Adults enter into the dramatic events which happen to children, therefore we should not leave them out of the dramatic events portrayed on the screen. We need, therefore, to develop experimentally the production of motion pictures which are artistically, educationally, and hygienically sound for children.

Finally, we must look forward to the time when the art of the masses—the motion picture—is not under the domination of commercial interests. The tremendous power to influence men's minds, inherent in the motion picture, must not rest in the hands of any single group of persons, no matter how high-minded or unselfish they may be. The final criterion for motion-picture content ought not to be "Can we make money from it?" but "Does it make life richer, more meaningful, more enjoyable?"

Our major present need is not for escape literature or drama. Instead, we need in the arts a vigorous handling of social realities. We need sensitive poets, dramatists, scenarists, men with artistic integrity who can view the current scene with clarity and insight and present us their findings in gripping, dramatic form.

They must include in their purview the major problems that beset children, youth, and adults when these involve material that can be dramatically presented. No human problem which is fitted to the motion-picture medium ought to be excluded from the screen. The motion-picture screen, a parade of life and manners, should be a study of conduct, honestly, dramatically, and entertainingly presented.

APPENDIX

231

INDEX